FOOD FOR MOOD

a CoolTan Arts cookbook

Published by CoolTan Books 2013
Unit B, 237 Walworth Road, London SE17 1RL

A CIP catalogue record for this book is available at the British Library

This project was realised with the support of the Peter Minet Trust and Guy's and St Thomas' Charity

ISBN 978-0-9524190-2-0
COOLTAN ARTS
www.cooltanarts.org.uk

Photographs and art works by contributors
Edited by Elizabeth Cochrane
Designed and typeset by Cecilia Bonilla
Printed and bound by C&C Offset Printing Co., Ltd

MIX
Paper from responsible sources
FSC® C008047

This book is dedicated to the memory of Peter Detre, with love and thanks for all his inspiration and support.

Peter was a mentor to CoolTan Arts from 2007 until his untimely death in 2011, through Pilotlight, a charity that teams business people with the charitable sector. Peter had a way with words, and knew how to use them to enable CoolTan Arts to put its message across to the people with the purses. He was also famous for his love of cooking.

Contents

Kitchen Artistry

Feast Days

Feeding the Village

Sweet Treats

Cup of Joy

Foreword

by Rosemary Shrager

When I was filming my TV show 'School for Cooks' I was sitting outside while everyone was making fish soup in the kitchen and the flavours and smells were coming out to me. I don't know what it is – it's like warmth really, that enjoyment of smelling food and loving it. It's nothing to do with being greedy. It has to come from the heart – a passion inside you. I just love the enthusiasm people show when they enjoy food.

For the first half of my life cooking was my hobby – I did it because I loved it. In the second half of my life, the emphasis changed: apart from loving it, my hobby became my business. In one week I lost everything when my husband's business went under, and I had to put food on my table. I had nothing except my talent, my experience and my friends. The most important thing for me was not to look back. If I'd looked back I could not have gone forward, so I just had to get on with the job.

All my life I've written, drawn pictures, putting ideas down. That's how I work. I didn't go to cookery school but I did go to art college. I learned to love colour, shape, texture and feel, and combinations of all of these, and this is what I now like to bring to a plate of food. I want to see a beautiful picture on a plate. However, flavour is still paramount, of course. I start with the background of my culinary picture, adding the layers and refinements as I go until there is a rich, woven togetherness, which I hope will make for a wonderful dish. Sometimes I literally dream up recipes at night, sometimes I am fired by a sudden idea and experiment until I find what I consider the very best way of putting it into practice.

I am passionate about cooking. It is in my blood, like an adrenaline rush. Whether I am cooking or painting I find creation a form of escapism. It can actually take you into another dimension. It can be so engaging that you forget about the past and the future, time completely disappears, and you can just be yourself, giving your feelings and thoughts a form, and clarifying your ideas. It can be really calming and energising. I don't think people have so much time these days to cook and they can't always be bothered. It's a big mistake though. You can have so much fun through cooking, and it can generate laughter, friendship and camaraderie.

I am so delighted to have been asked to introduce the CoolTan Arts cookbook, and to be involved with this small, inspirational charity which is achieving such marvellous results in its community. It is wonderful that people have a chance to expand and strengthen themselves, their dreams and their identities, through this vital access to creativity. It is fantastic that they can do this in an environment of passion, love and hope. It is so important. I fully support CoolTan Arts and the commitment of the staff and volunteers who make it possible. I wish all luck to everybody involved in CoolTan Arts and the CoolTan Arts cookbook. Enjoy!

Introduction

We all have to eat: food is an intrinsic part of each day for people around the globe, no matter what their circumstances are or what society they're part of. It's something we all experience, and so it connects us to each other. The sheer number of recipes contributed for this cookbook shows how important food is to people. At the same time, what we eat reflects our separate cultures. The reasons for eating certain things and the ways that we treat food vary from place to place, and this means that in preparing, eating and sharing food we express something about who we are and where we're from.

How we feel about food also reflects our individual histories, the way we were brought up, and food has a spiritual significance for many people, whether within a religious context or in a more personal way. Many of the recipes here are accompanied by personal stories: memories of childhood or significant events, reflections on the pleasure that cooking can bring.

There are hundreds of theories about the effect of various food types and eating regimes upon our bodies and our minds, and although the science has not been fully investigated, it's clear that how and what we eat has an enormous effect on our mental health. In the end, the most important thing is that we should be able to enjoy our food. It's a way to look after ourselves by providing our bodies with nutrients, but also just by treating ourselves with care. Creativity also has powerful benefits for mental health, and we hope that the variety of dishes collected here will inspire you to try new things.

With this project we are celebrating the creativity of cooking, the comfort of nostalgia, the conviviality and warmth that comes with sharing food together, and the cultural exchange that becomes possible through enjoying different cuisines. All the recipes, articles and photographs have been contributed by participants, staff, volunteers, mentors, trustees and friends of CoolTan Arts.

Cooking without much equipment

A well-stocked kitchen might have all kinds of gadgets, utensils, pots and pans, but it's quite easy to make do with just a few basic items. You'll certainly need one saucepan and one frying pan, a couple of bowls, a wooden spoon, a sharp knife and a chopping board. Keep your eyes open for unexpected cheap solutions: you can find very cheap bamboo steamers in Asian supermarkets, for example (you just balance them over a pot of boiling water). Don't forget to look in charity shops, which often carry kitchen goods, or at jumble sales.

You can get by fairly easily without measuring scales, as in most cases (except when baking) estimated quantities are fine: for dry ingredients, see how much the whole packet of food is supposed to weigh and then use what looks like a half or a quarter, as relevant. If you don't have a measuring cup, it might be worth figuring out which of your smaller mugs is about the right size – and then you can always use that as your guide.

The microwave can be used for much more than you might think. It's actually very good for making casserole-style dishes, rice pudding: anything that doesn't need much stirring or browning. Fish is excellent cooked in the microwave – just go carefully so you don't overdo it and dry it out. A piece of salmon or haddock is cooked through as soon as it has turned opaque.

If you're short of space, save your sanity by cleaning up as you go and consider doing all the preparation (vegetable-chopping, egg-beating, cheese-grating etc.) before you start. That helps to keep things orderly. If you only have one burner, or one pot, lots of sauces can be prepared first and set aside before making the rice, pasta or whatever else they're going with. See the one-pot recipes in the Kitchen Artistry chapter.

Your kitchen shelf

Here, for inspiration, is a list of spices and other oddments you might keep on your kitchen shelf. You can add other things, depending on your cooking habits, and you can be inventive with what you've got, too: sometimes a typical English or other European dish can be made more interesting by adding a pinch of curry or cumin powder. Keep dried ingredients in airtight containers to preserve their flavour.

Of course you don't need to have all of this. Working through some recipes from this book will mean that you gradually acquire a few different things. If you're wondering where to start, however, you could make sure you have salt and pepper, either cumin or garam masala, chilli in some form and oregano or mixed herbs, along with some light vegetable oil and low-salt stock powder, plain flour, tomato paste (or purée) and fresh garlic and lemons. It doesn't need to be complicated.

powdered spices: curry powder, garam masala, turmeric, garlic, pepper, cumin, coriander, cayenne, cinnamon, chilli, allspice, cloves, nutmeg

spice seeds: coriander, cumin, methi, mustard, fennel, anise, caraway, peppercorns

dried herbs: whole bay leaves, whole curry leaves, rosemary, mint, thyme, oregano, sage, tarragon, dill (note: delicate leaves like parsley, basil and coriander don't keep their flavour so well when dried)

also dried: cinnamon bark, cardamom pods, saffron strands, star anise, chilli flakes, sesame seeds, poppy seeds

herbs in pots on the windowsill: try parsley, sage, thyme, basil, rosemary, chives

other powders: arrowroot (a good thickener), vegetable stock powder, baking soda, baking powder, cocoa powder

salts: table salt, sea-salt, crystal (also known as Himalayan) salt

oils: vegetable or groundnut oil, olive oil, ghee

pastes: tomato, garlic, tahini, creamed coconut, tamarind, various curry pastes

bottles: vanilla essence, soy sauce or tamari, Worcestershire sauce, white wine vinegar, Balsamic vinegar

flours: plain flour, gram (chickpea) flour, rice flour, cornflour for thickening

sugars: granulated white, soft brown, caster for baking, jaggery for Asian cooking

fruits: dried mango, tamarind, dates, raisins and sultanas

nuts: almonds – whole and flaked, cashews, walnuts, peanuts

tins: tomatoes, chickpeas, kidney beans, other peas, beans and lentils

jars: mustard, honey, molasses, various pickles and chutneys

fresh, in a basket: onions, garlic, lemons, fresh green chillies

dried: rice, lentils, beans, pasta

Note on quantities, weights and measures

An onion can be the size of a satsuma or a grapefruit, so when a recipe says 1 onion, you may wonder which onion to use! The answer is that unless it's specified it doesn't matter. Most recipes are pretty forgiving where quantity is concerned, and you can go with what you've got or what you prefer. Indeed, some of the recipes (e.g. colcannon, the salads) make a virtue of that.

As for weights and measures, we've stuck to metric – alongside pinches, splashes and handfuls, which can all be improvised. Note that a 'cup' is actually a specific measurement of volume, being 225 ml. Officially, a teaspoonful is 5 ml and a tablespoon is 15 ml. You may want to know that 1 lb is 454 g, so half a pound (8 oz) is roughly 250 g, and 1 pint is just over half a litre at 568 ml.

We do specify how many servings you will get from each recipe, but appetites vary, so this can only be approximate. If you have leftovers, you can freeze or refrigerate them for later, or turn them into something else (a soup, say, or a filling for pancakes or for baked potato). And if the worst happens and there isn't enough food for the number of hungry people, give them bowls of nuts, a mini tinned-soup starter, and loads of bread and butter on the side... and use smaller plates!

Cooking and mental health

Anyone who's got less energy than usual – because of illness, medication, or an emotionally demanding phase of life – can find it hard to summon the motivation for proper cooking. The effort needed for washing up dishes can put you off starting to cook at all, and sometimes it can feel demotivating if your cooking facilities are very basic. Eating sardines from the tin, or a few dry crackers to stave off the worst of hunger, is not too bad for you nutritionally, but eating too little can be a problem for some people, and turning always to the same unhealthy but simple options is a temptation for others. In order to eat a balanced diet, we need to find ways to get over these difficulties: simple ways to make ourselves feel better, and to create real meals with a minimum of effort.

One excellent trick to make your life easier is using basic foods that become pre-prepared ingredients, such as frozen vegetables, tins of ready-flavoured chopped tomato, or tinned soups that work as delicious sauces. Frozen veg are easy to use, and can be just as good for you nutritionally as fresh veg, if not better: they are usually frozen so quickly after picking that the vitamins have no chance to degrade.

Even more simply, you can just add extra ingredients, whether fresh or frozen, to a ready-made dish. They will give it more bulk, enrich the taste, and help you easily do something nice for yourself. Tinned beans and chickpeas can be added to almost anything with a sauce, and flavourings like chilli or Worcestershire sauce, Maggi liquid seasoning or mustard can really lift a meal – especially one you've eaten many times before.

Over time, poor eating can make you more depressed, and harm your physical health too. A healthy diet, on the other hand, can improve your mood. If you can't manage a full meal, small frequent snacks are ok: try cereal and milk, toast with peanut butter, rice pudding, fresh fruit, or tinned fruit with yoghurt or evaporated milk. A sandwich of cheese, tinned fish or meat on wholemeal bread with a bit of salad, or something on toast, like baked beans or an egg, are very good. If you have a microwave, a jacket potato is an easy hot meal. Nuts and raisins are healthy and easy to eat.

If you really can't face food, have a hot milky drink. And if you know you're not eating properly, take a multivitamin and mineral supplement. There is some evidence that omega-3 fats, as found in oily fish, can help improve mood. A good intake of fruit and vegetables may also help. Don't forget to drink enough fluid: even slight dehydration may affect your mood.

Sharing food

You may find it easier to eat with other people. In fact, if you ask people what they think makes food count as 'a meal', one of the most common answers is 'eating with somebody else'. For some reason, we don't accord the same importance to food that we consume alone. This is a shame, given that feeding yourself can be a means of expressing kindness towards yourself, and a constructive step towards good mental and physical health. One way to overcome a tendency towards self-neglect is suggested in Ari Henry's A Meal for One, in the Feast Days chapter.

Sharing food represents friendliness, conviviality and love. It's a wonderful thing to be motivated to put special effort into a meal because you will be giving something to someone else. And we can celebrate this with a simple experience like splitting an apple into quarters and handing it around, putting a couple of biscuits onto a small plate to honour a guest, or boiling up extra rice or potatoes to make a meal for one stretch to feed two.

STARTOUT RIGHT

Whatever time you eat breakfast, celebrate the day.
A plate of fruit or a full cooked meal can put you on the
right track for health and happiness.

How important is breakfast to you?

"It's great if I can manage it, not the end of the world if I can't."

*"Nigerians believe that food is important to the overall wellbeing of
an individual: this is why we habitually take a good breakfast before
leaving home every day – so that we can cope with hard work, whether
it's farming, driving, cleaning, security work or office work. A good
breakfast starts you off in a good mood. My personal experience has
shown that when I take a good breakfast the chances are that I'm more
stable and focussed and achieve more during working days than when I
don't. I get weak, tired and grumpy when I haven't had a good breakfast."*

*"Breakfast is really important for me. I'm a raw foodie, so I have
fruit salads mainly for my breakfast: usually a banana, persimmon,
pomegranate, cherries or grapes, with raw nuts like almonds, brazils,
cashews – sometimes topped with honey."*

"I rarely eat breakfast. When I do, then I skip lunch: I find both too much."

*"Breakfast is a luxury. Usually I don't have time for it, and just grab
something on the way. But whenever I find the chance to sit down to it,
say during the weekend at home with family and friends (or, especially
wonderful, with a friend in a café), breakfast is a true celebration of the day."*

Bread Rolls

from Andrew Black

This is a useful recipe for when I am around the house most of the day but can't settle at anything. Sometimes I will start making rolls in a fit of enthusiasm then forget about them, or realise I need to go out before they are finished. The kneading gets rid of any pent up tension: you can take your frustrations out on the dough!

500 ml hand-hot water
(or half milk if available)

2 tsp dried yeast

1 tsp sugar

125 g margarine

500 g strong white flour

500 g strong brown flour
(or specialist flour)

- Mix the water, sugar and yeast and leave it for at least half an hour.

- Mix the margarine with the flour in a large mixing bowl and then add the yeast mixture and mix again.

- Knead the dough on a working surface, then put it back in a bowl and leave it in a warm place for at least an hour. Meanwhile, prepare two baking trays.

- Knead the dough again, and divide it into 24 rolls (I divide it into 3 and then each of the 3 bits into 8). Roll each 'blob' between your hands and place on a baking tray.

- Leave for 30 minutes or longer to let rise again. Turn on the oven and let it heat up to 245 °C / gas mark 8 (or 220 °C in a fan oven).

- Bake the rolls for 15 minutes or until done. Take them off the baking try and let cool on a wire cooling tray.

Note: You can freeze the cooked rolls.

Perfect Scrambled Eggs

There is nothing more comforting or more enticing than a mound of light fluffy scrambled eggs, glistening with butter, on top of some hot, crunchy toast. It's the food of childhood, of lazy Sunday mornings, of recuperating after an illness or a big night out.

How to avoid a dry rubbery mess? The key is to follow three basic but essential rules:

1: Use the best and freshest eggs you can – ideally good quality free-range organic eggs.

2: Do not stint on the butter! (For a lower-fat option, consider poached eggs instead.)

3: The most important. Be patient. Scrambled eggs are slow food.

- Before you start cooking you need to prepare a couple of things. Put the slices of bread in the toaster, and have your plates standing by.

- Crack the eggs into a bowl (2 per person) and beat well with a pinch of salt.

- Heat either a small non-stick frying pan or a small heavy-bottomed saucepan on a low heat – very low. When you put in your butter (about a tablespoon) it should melt slowly: if it's too quick and your pan is too hot, the butter will burn and your eggs will become rubbery. If you think it is too hot just remove the pan from the heat for a couple of minutes to let it cool.

- When the butter has melted, pour in the eggs and begin to stir, slowly working from the outside and folding in. It will take between 6 and 10 minutes for them to scramble. They should not be left alone for more than 10 seconds at a time and, once again, be patient.

- Start the toast 5 minutes in and it will be ready in time.

- The eggs should still be slightly liquid when you remove them from the heat. Add a final knob of butter to arrest the cooking process. Quickly butter the toast, and top with your finished eggs and a twist of black pepper.

Note: For variety, try adding different flavours, for example the following:

Stir in a tablespoon of crème fraîche once the eggs are cooked and top with some chopped chives. Best served on wholewheat toast.

Chop up some chorizo sausage (or similar) and a green pepper, lightly fry them in oil and have them ready to stir into the final mixture. Sprinkle with a handful of finely chopped parsley.

Lay strips of smoked salmon over a toasted, buttered bagel and top with your eggs and some chopped chives.

Very simply, a little chopped fresh sage is delicious with eggs. It's also a very easy herb to grow on your windowsill.

Fruity Porridge

Porridge makes a warming, cosy winter breakfast and is one of the healthiest foods you can eat. It's much cheaper and more nutritious than breakfast cereal, which is often highly processed and full of sugar. Oats contain essential fatty acids that may be beneficial to brain function and folic acid, a vitamin that may help prevent depression. Dried fruit can be a good source of vitamin C, fibre and iron. A bowl of porridge in the morning will boost your energy levels throughout the day.

(serves 1)

½ cup porridge oats

1 cup milk (or water)

a handful of chopped raisins or other dried fruit

- Put the oats, milk and dried fruit into a saucepan.

- Bring to the boil and then simmer gently until thickened.

- Serve warm, with seeds or fresh berries if you like.

- For an unusual twist, try adding cinnamon and lemon zest to the mixture.

Breakfast Arepas

These corn patties make a delicious savoury breakfast. You can serve them with fried or scrambled eggs, fresh white cheese and black beans, or chopped fresh avocados and tomatoes mixed with lime juice, chillies and fresh coriander.

pre-cooked corn flour (see note)
water
salt
spring onions or fresh coriander, finely chopped (optional)

- Measure out 1 cup of flour per person; add 1 cup of water per cup of flour. Add a touch of salt and any extras you like: finely sliced spring onions or herbs, for example.

- Mix the ingredients until they form a soft, pliant dough that's not too sticky. Let it rest for about 5 minutes: not too long, or it will get stiff. If it looks like it needs more water – wait! Only add a little more if it is breaking apart easily after resting.

- Gently form small balls from the mixture and flatten into discs about the size of the palm of your hand. (You can cover and refrigerate the discs for a few hours if you like.)

- Heat a little oil in a large frying pan and cook the arepas in batches until they're golden brown: about 5 minutes on one side, then 3 minutes on the other side.

Note: Pre-cooked corn flour should be found in any shop selling South American products, and will be labelled harina precocida or masarepa, and have the words "harina de maiz refinada precocida" (meaning refined, precooked corn flour) on the package. Don't confuse it with cornstarch, which is just a thickening agent.

Break Free From Breakfast

Sandhya Kaffo

There is a myriad of opinions, suggestions and guidelines concerning how, when and what to eat: modern health specialists' rules and the various laws of 'ancient wisdom' take into account your constitution, your blood type, the weather, your state of mind, culture, lifestyle and so on: the list goes on to the point of dizziness.

So, for example, many argue that breakfast is the most important meal of the day, and indeed one saying calls for us to "eat breakfast like a king, lunch like a prince, and dinner like a pauper". However, there's also a viewpoint that we should eat as our ancestors did: hunter-gatherers might not have eaten breakfast at all and supper would have been the most important meal of the day. The traditional Chinese medicine food cycle proposes that the stomach is in peak condition to eat between 7 am and 9 am, but the Ayurvedic dosha cycle suggests 10 am–2 pm.

All the rules may be true, but the question is, which one is true for you? The teacher I had for my Master's study in nutrition used to say we have to "become our own petri-dish", which in essence means we have to become our own researcher and establish what is right for us as unique individuals when it comes to food. Ultimately we should be intuitive about how we eat. If we match our food to our needs, we can elevate our mood to where we want it to be. Failure to do so can lead to an unhealthy attitude towards food on a mental, emotional and physical level.

Paying attention to others' opinions instead of our own can send us into spin. I say, feel your body and feed it what it needs. The body is a dynamic living thing and it needs a watchful eye. Nurturing one's mood goes beyond food.

'Like Yoghurt' Breakfast Recipe

from Sandhya Kaffo

This is an example of how easy and therapeutic it can be to engage in the joyful process of creative food preparation.

My husband's usual breakfast routine is to mix a home-made fresh fruit compote with thick plain goat's yoghurt and add some dried fruit & nut muesli to it. He makes 4 tubs at a time and leaves them in the fridge to soak and soften. Late one evening, he exclaimed that he had forgotten to buy any yoghurt and therefore would not have anything to take to work for breakfast. He totally overlooked the fact that there were still fruits and muesli! So I took out the dried wild blueberries and dates that we had and soaked them overnight. In the morning I got up and put together this tub of 'like yoghurt' breakfast. Here is the very simple recipe from which many variations can be made. You will need two empty yoghurt pots, a mixing bowl and – ideally – a blender.

a handful of dried fruits – use whatever you have available,
e.g. dates and wild blueberries

fruit soaking water – approximately 3 cups

2 level cups fruit & nut muesli

fresh fruits, chopped – again whatever you have to hand,
e.g. 2 small pears, 1 banana, 1 lime

- Soak your dried fruits in water overnight.

- In the morning, put the soaked dried fruits into the blender along with the water from soaking and the fresh fruit (here I am using chopped pear and banana, with the juice of a lime). Pulse the blender in short bursts until you have a nicely textured fruit mix.

- Place the muesli in the mixing bowl and add the fruit mix, then stir together thoroughly and leave the muesli to soak up all the moisture (the longer you leave it, the softer and mushier it gets).

- Scoop it into yoghurt pots and leave it in fridge till you're ready to eat it.

- If the mixture is too thick, add some fruit juice.

Note: You can also add a bit of yoghurt to this recipe for variation, or use the fruit and muesli mix as a topping for a bowlful of yoghurt.

Moussaka

Potato Pancakes

Ghalieh Esfanaaj

Spinach and Potato in Cream Sauce

Fried Chicken Livers

Potato Salad

Egg and Onion

Barley Soup

Pepe Soup

Cook-Down Jerk Chicken

Spiced Couscous with Roasted Aubergines and Peppers

Kartoffelsuppe with Apple Pancakes

TASTE OF HOME

Tastes and aromas evoke moments from our past, reminding us of childhood, people we love, and where we come from. With food, we can connect to our history, make memories real, and express our heritage.

Moussaka

from Steven Hampson (and Andreas Phiphollou)

Moussaka is something I've liked since I was a child. My father often made this dish for my brother and me. If I had a bad day at school, for instance doing cross-country running, which I hated and which usually induced a state of depression in me, the thought of a good supper was a real comfort. I knew I could endure the day with the promise of something that would have an uplifting effect on me, and erase the despair of the morning. To this day, moussaka evokes happy snapshots of my childhood. My recollections, many of them good, can be restored through enjoying this meal and it's as though they were immortalised on film. This recipe is something my father used to make, but I would also like to mention my beloved late mother, Olive. Her influence lives on in my cooking and my day-to-day existence.

(serves 8)

3 medium aubergines, peeled and thinly sliced

vegetable or sunflower oil

450 g potatoes, thinly sliced

450 g courgettes, thinly sliced lengthways

1 green pepper, de-seeded and sliced

2 artichoke hearts, sliced (optional)

1 large onion, chopped

4 cloves of garlic, crushed

900 g minced beef (or lamb or pork)

100 ml water

1 level tsp ground cinnamon

1 cup finely chopped parsley

1 tbsp tomato purée

2 tomatoes, peeled and chopped

2 tomatoes, sliced

2 tbsp grated parmesan or cheddar cheese

salt and freshly ground pepper

For the topping:

40 g butter

100 ml vegetable or sunflower oil

110 g plain four

1.15 litres (2 pints) milk

3 tbsp grated parmesan or cheddar cheese

pinch of salt

- Before you begin, put the aubergines into a colander and sprinkle with salt. Place a plate on top and leave to drain for 30 minutes. Rinse and dry with kitchen paper.

- Pre-heat the oven to 200 °C / gas mark 6.

- Heat some oil in a large frying pan and lightly brown the potatoes on both sides. Remove and set aside. Then, in turn, lightly brown the courgettes, aubergines, green pepper and artichoke hearts in the same way. Place the vegetables in a colander, or pat with kitchen paper, to get rid of any excess oil.

- Fry the onion and garlic until brown. Then add the minced beef, brown it, add the water and continue cooking over a medium heat for 10–15 minutes, stirring occasionally. Then add the chopped tomatoes, tomato purée, cinnamon, parsley and a seasoning of salt and pepper. Stir well and switch off the heat.

- Arrange half of the potatoes over the base of a deep ovenproof dish. Then place half of the courgettes, aubergines, green pepper and artichokes over the top together with one sliced tomato. Sprinkle on half of the cheese, then spread the meat mixture over the top, layer on the rest of the vegetables and sprinkle with the remaining cheese.

- For the topping, heat the butter and the oil. With a wooden spoon, stir in the flour and cook gently for a few minutes. Gradually pour in the milk, stirring continuously to avoid any lumps, and simmering until thickened. Then add a pinch of salt and stir in the cheese, reserving a little to sprinkle over the top.

- Pour the sauce over the vegetables and sprinkle the remaining cheese over the top. Bake for about 45 minutes or until golden brown. Leave to stand for 10 minutes before cutting into squares and serving with a green salad.

Note: You can actually prepare moussaka a day in advance and just pop it into the hot oven an hour before you need it.

Learning To Cook

"I can't remember learning to cook. I guess I watched my mum and followed on from there. At 11, I was making spaghetti bolognese and bean stew for my family. I was a very responsible child!"

"My first cooking memory is of making omelettes on my own. I've no idea how old I was, but I was experimenting with food colouring and I gave a purple omelette to the cat."

"I'm not sure I can cook! I do remember calling my grandmother when I was in my first year of university because I needed advice on how to cook rice. I learned by watching my mother. After moving out of home, I just continued to live on home-made food."

"I learned cooking in my student days when I was living in a hostel where many people cooked food for themselves. We had a group called GGG, meaning the Good Grub Group. I was part of them for years."

Potato Pancakes

from Zbigniew Podziewski

As a 6-year-old boy I loved to watch my mum making these in the kitchen, and I assumed that the spectacles she was wearing were just for eye protection – because frying the pancakes always caused hot oil to be splashed everywhere. Can you imagine how surprised she was when I asked her to lend me her glasses because I wanted to do some shallow frying? Bear in mind kitchen hazards, but do be brave and make potato pancakes!

(serves 8)

2 kg baking potatoes

3 big onions

100 g diced bacon

2–3 heaped tbsp flour

marjoram

salt and black pepper

2 eggs (optional)

- Peel the potatoes, then grate them using the finest grater.

- Grate two of the onions and mix them in with the potatoes.

- Dice the third onion with and fry it with the bacon, then mix that into the potato and raw onion mixture. (The fried onion gives a richer taste, but can be omitted.)

- Add the flour, a few pinches of marjoram, black pepper and a pinch of salt.

- Feel free to add eggs to help the mixture bind, if you like.

- Form into pancakes and fry on both sides in shallow oil until brown.

- Serve with yoghurt, or sour cream mixed with cottage cheese and a tiny pinch of salt.

Ghalieh Esfanaaj

from Ramin Farajpour

Ghalieh Esfanaaj is a very nutritious Persian (i.e. Iranian) dish of spinach with little meatballs. I remember my mother cooking it for me along with spinach and potato in cream sauce. As a child I used to love the taste and smell of spinach: when I got back from school and smelled it I would know that my mother was cooking one of these two dishes.

(serves 4)

50 g dried black-eyed beans

50 g dried split peas

50 g dried brown lentils

1 onion

250–300 g minced lamb or beef

salt and black pepper

vegetable oil

500 g fresh spinach

¼ tsp pomegranate powder

100 g fresh mint or 1½ tbsp dried mint

1 cup kashk (thick fermented whey – you can use sour cream instead)

- Wash the black-eyed beans and soak overnight, or in warm water for a minimum of 4 hours. Rinse and drain them, then place them in a large pan with the split peas and lentils and approximately 1 litre of water. Add a little salt and cook over a medium heat for 20 minutes, until just soft. About one cup (225 ml) of water should be left in the pan at this stage. You can add extra water or ladle some out if necessary.

- Peel and grate or finely chop the onion. If you grate it, squeeze out as much moisture as you can, otherwise the meatballs won't bind together. Add the onion to the minced meat with a little salt and black pepper, and mix well. Shape the mixture into small balls (the size of walnuts) and fry them in vegetable oil over a medium heat until they are lightly browned all over.

- Wash the spinach and drain well, then chop finely. Put it together with the black-eyed beans, split peas, lentils and meatballs, and cook this all over a low heat for

15–20 minutes until the pulses are soft and there is no water left. Add the pomegranate powder to the pot for the last minute of cooking.

- Wash the mint and chop finely. Fry it in oil for a couple of minutes. If you are using dried mint, just heat the oil, add the dried mint and take it off the heat immediately, as dried herbs quickly burn.

- Serve Ghalieh Esfanaaj in 4 bowls with a quarter of the kashk (about 4 spoonfuls) and a quarter of the mint on the top of each. Serve with a good flat bread or plain rice.

Notes: You can find pomegranate powder in Indian shops (where it may be called anardana powder) as well as in Iranian shops. If you get stuck, you could replace it with tamarind or amchoor (mango) powder, which are both similarly tart.

As an alternative to soaking the beans overnight, you can boil them for 2 minutes, then leave to soak in the hot water for 1 hour.

Spinach and Potato in Cream Sauce

from Ramin Farajpour

This Persian side dish is delicious as an accompaniment to chicken or other white meat or fish.

(serves 3–4)

30 g butter

1 medium onion, chopped

2 tbsp flour

¼ tsp salt

¾ tsp white pepper

500 ml milk

100 ml single cream

1 tsp dried parsley

200 g fresh spinach, chopped

3 large potatoes, cut into rounds

5 tbsp fresh parsley, finely chopped

60 g cheddar cheese, grated

- Pre-heat the oven to 180 °C / gas mark 4.

- To make the white sauce, melt two thirds of the butter in a pan, add the onion and sauté it for 2 minutes. Add the flour and cook it for a minute, stirring, until the flour turns lightly brown. Add the pepper and salt and then gradually add the milk, stirring continuously to avoid lumps. When the sauce thickens, add the cream and dried parsley and take it off the heat.

- In a separate pan, melt the remaining butter, add the spinach and sauté it for 5 minutes, then take it off the heat. You should end up with 1 cup of cooked spinach.

- Fry the potatoes in vegetable oil for 5–10 minutes and drain on kitchen paper.

- Add the spinach and fried potato rounds to the white sauce, spread the mixture in an oven-proof baking dish and sprinkle the fresh parsley and the cheddar cheese on top.

- Bake for 20 minutes.

Fried Chicken Livers

You can buy packs of chicken livers very cheaply in local markets such as Brixton Market. The butcher should already have removed the gall bladders (greenish in colour) but double check, and if you find any traces, remove them and wash the livers properly.

(serves 2)

1 small onion

green chilli

pinch of mustard seeds

pinch of jeera (cumin) seeds

200 g chicken livers

- Chop the onion into small pieces and add chopped green chilli to taste.

- Heat some oil in a pan, put in a few mustard seeds and a pinch of jeera (cumin) seeds, then after a few seconds add the onion and chilli and fry gently.

- When the onion is almost cooked, add the livers and cook for a further 5–10 minutes, until they're just cooked through.

- You can serve these in wraps with salad, or mix with rice for a tasty pilaff.

Edible Walks

Maggie Jay

There is a bountiful amount of wild fruits, vegetables and herbs in Southwark. For example, Chumleigh Gardens contains a treasure trove behind the new cafe: there are grapes, pomegranates, apples, pears and berries, in shades of blue, orange and red. Here the community discover local Southwark produce by foraging, scrumping and generally rummaging about in shrubbery.

Organisations such as Pickling Peckham (who have a particular interest in preserving fruit and vegetables and work as part of the Abundance project network) promote local people's involvement with the environment, enriching diets and developing the outdoor lives of residents in a famously deprived inner city borough. They show what can be done with local 'wild' or unused crops even deep within the urban jungle. The process can also forge strong community bonds.

There is a huge amount of free food growing on our doorstep. Pickling Peckham and others demonstrate a need for a better thought-out approach to the planting, harvesting and use of food and other crops in our parks and estates. Part of the vision is to see more orchard trees and edible hedgerows in Southwark spaces – offering affordable and sustainable access to seasonal, local food.

In addition to sharing meaningful practical skills, such community projects encourage people to value their environment, to develop an awareness of the seasons and an interest in plants so that we see them in a new way. They are planting metaphorical seeds, as it were, because it only takes a tiny thing – someone showing you a fascinating flower, a child digging up potatoes, the smell of fresh thyme bringing back a memory – to inspire an abiding hobby that cannot be beaten for its eco credentials, economic and health benefits, and therapeutic value.

Potato Salad

from Michelle Baharier

This is best made with new potatoes, which makes it a summer dish. You do not peel the potatoes, just scrub them before cooking. This was a dish my Dad loved: we grew potatoes in the compost heap in our garden. The herbs are easy to grow too, and the dill in particular gives a wonderful flavour – one we could use more often.

(serves 3–4)

½ kg new potatoes

1 medium onion

2–3 spring onions

4 radishes, chopped thinly (use the English red globe variety)

handful of dill, finely chopped

handful of mint leaves, finely chopped

handful of fresh chives, finely chopped

½ a jar of mayonnaise

pinch of sea salt, ground

ground black pepper

pinch of cayenne pepper (optional)

- Scrub the potatoes (you can buy potato scrubbing bushes from hardware shops), then rinse and cut into 2 cm chunks.

- Place the potato pieces in a pan of cold water, bring to the boil and simmer till just soft (you should just be able to pierce them with a fork). Be careful as over-cooked potatoes go floury and fall apart. Then rinse them in cold water till cold.

- Meanwhile, dice the onions and place them in a medium-sized bowl. I like Spanish onions because they make your eyes water and are hotter than most, but you may prefer a red onion, which is milder and adds attractive colour to the dish.

- Slice the radishes and spring onions finely, using both white and green parts of the spring onions, and add those.

- Add the herbs and mayonnaise, season lightly and mix well.

Egg and Onion

from Michelle Baharier

This is a Jewish dish which I learnt from my Mum and used to have to make when I worked on a bagel stall in Wembley market on Sundays. It's one of the best simple things to eat that you can imagine.

(serves 2)

4 free-range eggs

1 medium onion, either white or red

2–4 spring onions

small handful of dill, finely chopped

knob of butter, softened

4 tbsp mayonnaise

salt and black pepper to taste

- Boil the eggs in a pan for 8–10 minutes.

- Chop the onions and spring onions and mix them together in a bowl. Add the dill.

- When the eggs are cooked, let them cool, peel the shells off and dice them. Add to the onions with a knob of butter and the mayonnaise.

- Mix everything together until you have a wonderful paste, season it, and serve on toast or in bagels.

Barley Soup

from Michelle Baharier

My upbringing made soup a special feature in my life, as I come from a Jewish family. Chicken soup then was fundamental to our weekly diet (I no longer eat it but instead make my own veggie version with wheat-free matzo balls). Less common is this barley soup, which I want to share because it reminds me of home, of my mum and of being a child. I remember being about 7, coming in from the rain, my mum being home and this wonderful smell wafting though our house. Although originally made with meat, the version I make is completely vegan, and very simple. It's a wonderful winter warmer.

(serves 4–6)

1 medium Spanish onion, chopped

3 medium carrots, peeled and diced

1 small swede, peeled and diced

3 parsnips, peeled and diced

3 medium potatoes, peeled and diced

1 cup pearl barley

pinch of salt

pinch of red and black pepper

- It is preferable to cook this in a pressure cooker as the barley will cook better that way. However if you don't have one it will just take a bit longer. Put all the ingredients in a saucepan, well covered with water, and bring to the boil. Then turn the heat down and simmer for about 35–50 minutes until the vegetables and barley are soft. In a pressure cooker it should take about 20 minutes.

- You can blend or mash it slightly before serving, or serve it with a spoon and a fork and let the person eating mash up their own vegetables.

- This can be served with tamari or soy sauce (instead of the salt). If you like, you can add additional toppings like grated cheese or chilli sauce.

Note: Pearl barley is barley processed to remove its hull and bran. Even without the bran, it's a nutritious food, containing B vitamins and various minerals. The vegetables in this dish are also full of nutrients.

Nigerian Food

Marie Johnson

West Africa has a variety of foods, of which maize or corn, cassava and yams, sweet potatoes and Irish potatoes are particularly common. We also have many vegetables and herbs which form a pretty important aspect of our nutrition and in my country, Nigeria, we really appreciate vegetables and herbs in our meals. Fruits also play an important part in the whole mix, and products tend to be seasonal, since a lot of our food is grown organically.

Pepe Soup

from Marie Johnson, volunteer manager at Southwark Muslim Women's Association

This is an African dish that is especially popular in Nigeria. It can be made with fish or meat. Although it has a mixture of spices it is very simple to prepare, and that is its beauty. It is peppery, hot and spicy and it is served with fufu (mashed cassava) or pounded yam. Pepper soup ('pepe soup' in Nigerian dialects) is eaten by everyone and often used to soothe mums who have just had a baby. When I am feeling hyperactive, I drink some pepe soup and it sends me to sleep! There is usually no oil in it, which makes it a very healthy dish. In Nigeria, it is seen as medicinal: if people feel ill and lose their appetite through childbearing, tiredness or malaria, they are often advised to avoid oily foods and take pepper soup for a couple of days. The amount of chilli pepper can be increased or decreased depending on the individual's level of tolerance.

You often find pepper soup in 'beer parlours', African-style restaurants, and local 'joints' and 'bukas' (both places to eat), as it is very popular in Nigeria. There are many varieties, as it can be made with almost any pieces of meat, including the entrails, skin and legs of goats or cows. In fact these days you can find chicken pepper soup, dry fish pepper soup or even lamb pepper soup. My favourite version is made with fish. Whichever type is eaten, it is a unique West African delicacy and Nigeria has made the eating of pepper soup very popular around the world.

(serves two)

½ a yam tuber

225 g beef or goat (preferably on the bone; fish can also be used)

1 fresh chilli pepper (a small round one, e.g. Scotch bonnet), finely chopped

1 onion, very finely chopped

4 cloves of garlic, finely chopped

1 whole Knorr (or other) seasoning cube

20 black peppercorns, crushed

pepper soup spice (optional)

- Cut the yam into 4 slices, wash, and then boil for 15 minutes until tender. Drain and leave aside to cool for a bit.

- Crumble the stock cube into 3 cups of water and add to the rest of the ingredients.

- Bring the soup to the boil, stir everything together, and leave to simmer until the meat is tender (maybe 20–30 minutes), but do not overcook.

- Mash or 'pound' or the yam and serve it with the pepe soup.

Notes: If you want to make this with fish, use catfish or any other firm, non-oily white fish. Boil all the other ingredients together first until the mix smells good, and only then add the fish. If you cook fish too long it falls apart!

If you are sensitive to chilli pepper, you can use less. Note that the spiciest part is the seeds. Pepper soup spice can be found in stores stocking Nigerian food, or sometimes – the best place – in a local market.

Shopping in Camberwell and Walworth

Steven Hampson

The local shops generally reflect the population living here. There are supermarkets that serve most of the community, but we also have a variety of other shops that serve the specific cultural needs of people who live here. We have large communities of Afro-Caribbeans, eastern Europeans, Chinese people and people of Arabic origin. We also have many people here from South America. If you walk through the market on East Street you will see a wide range of food that reflects the diversity of local inhabitants. You will see fruits and vegetables from Africa, South America and Asia. There are shops that specialise in eastern European food, for example many Polish shops that sell bread and other delicacies such as cakes and cold meats. Camberwell offers a real cultural feast: in theory you could eat something different every day.

Cook-Down Jerk Chicken

from Tichelle Norman

I'm from London. Now 23 years of age, I'm in my last year of studying for a fine art degree. My parents divorced when I was 6, but they still remain good friends, and they always support me. Whenever I stay at my daddy's he cooks this meal. He cuts the carrots big and chunky, the chicken is well browned and the gravy juice with all the lovely West Indian seasoning drenches the rice on my plate. I will always be his little girl.

(serves 3)

6–7 pieces of chicken (thighs, legs or a mixture)

1 lemon

3 large carrots

150–200g white long grain rice

For the seasoning:

splash of soy sauce

black pepper

jerk seasoning

Dunn's River all-purpose seasoning

pinch of thyme

2–3 onions, sliced

- Clean the chicken pieces with the lemon and remove any hairs, feather remnants or excess fat. Place them in a large bowl and add all the seasoning. (How much is entirely up to the cook's taste-buds: Daddy tends to use a fair amount of each!) Mix by hand so that the chicken is evenly covered, then leave aside for a while.

- Pour 3 spoonfuls of olive oil into a pot on a medium heat, place all the chicken pieces into the pot and let them cook for 2–3 minutes. Half-fill a drinking mug with cold water and pour this into the pot. Peel the carrots and slice them in rounds or lengthways, then add them to the pot. Leave it on a medium heat – covered – for an hour and a half, or longer if needed.

- About 15 minutes before the chicken's done, wash the rice and put it on to cook.

- Taste the chicken for seasoning, then serve it with the rice and salads or sliced tomatoes on the side of your plate.

Spiced Couscous with Roasted Aubergines and Peppers

from Sasha Dee

In India, couscous is often eaten as a snack at tea-time.

(serves 4)

350g (2 cups) couscous

2 aubergines

1 each of red, green and yellow peppers

1 tsp each of curry powder, garam masala, turmeric powder, chilli powder

1 tsp each of cumin seeds, coriander seeds, peppercorns, fennel seeds

1 cinnamon stick

2 bay leaves

To garnish:

½ a coconut, freshly grated

small handful of coriander leaves, finely chopped

2 or 3 small green chillies, finely chopped

- Prepare the couscous by placing in a tightly covered bowl with 1½ times the volume of boiling water or stock for 5–10 minutes.

- Roast the aubergines and the peppers in a moderately hot oven (about 190°C/gas mark 5) until the skins have started to break and a lovely cooked smell is coming out. This may take 45 minutes to an hour; turn the vegetables a couple of times during cooking.

- Meanwhile, heat 2 tablespoons of vegetable oil in a pan and put in the cumin and coriander seeds, peppercorns, fennel seeds and cinnamon stick. When they are jumping in the oil add the curry powder, garam masala, turmeric and chilli powder. Stir well.

- Add the steamed couscous, bay leaves and a pinch of salt to the spices and mix well. Put the lid on for a few minutes to let the flavours blend.

- To serve, dish the couscous out onto flat plates, dress it with the aubergines and peppers, and then garnish with grated coconut, chopped coriander and green chillies.

- You can also eat this with condiments like sweet mango chutney or pickles.

- Eat it while it is hot!

Kartoffelsuppe with Apple Pancakes

from Kathrin Kirrmann

This is a typical meal from the Black Forest region, which you probably wouldn't get in other parts of Germany. I love it, it's one of my favourite recipes from my mum and we often have it when I visit my parents in Germany. It may be a strange mix to eat potato soup and apple pancakes together. But it's delicious, good-mood food!

(serves 4)

For the soup:

800 g potatoes

pinch each of nutmeg, white pepper, salt

1 litre milk

200 ml single cream

For the apple pancakes:

250 g flour

500 ml milk

pinch of salt

4 eggs

4–5 apples

margarine for frying

sugar and cinnamon

- Peel the potatoes, quarter them, and cook in salted water until they are soft (approximately 20 minutes). Strain the potatoes and mash them in the cooking pan, adding nutmeg, white pepper and salt.

- Heat the milk and slowly stir it into the potatoes with the help of a hand mixer if you have one.

- At the end, add the cream, taste the soup and season again if necessary.

- To make the pancakes, mix the flour, milk, salt and eggs by hand or with a hand mixer until you have a soft batter. Let the batter rest for at least 15 minutes.

- Core and peel the apples, cut them into 2 mm-thick slices and put these into the batter.

- For each pancake, take a small spoonful of batter with 2–3 apple slices, put into a hot pan greased with a little margarine, and fry on both sides.

- Sprinkle sugar and cinnamon onto the pancakes and eat them with the potato soup.

COMFORT EATING

Food is a way to show you care. The simple act of cooking for someone else expresses love; you can also treat yourself kindly by giving your body what it needs.

Ghanaian Chicken in Peanut Sauce

from Liz Kalinauckas, 'host mum' in the Global Xchange volunteering programme

This is a family favourite – reminding us of our childhood in Kumasi, Ghana. It is an easy recipe to make and there's not much washing up, as it is made in one dish. We always have this meal when there is a family group of us – the taste just makes me feel comforted and happy to be round a table with my close family. I enjoy preparing everything and then whizzing all the sauce ingredients up together: individually they each have their own flavour but when they're all mixed together the taste is so delicious!

(serves 4–6)

a 1.75 kg chicken, skinned and jointed, or skinned chicken pieces

2 large onions, peeled and finely chopped

2 cloves of garlic, peeled and creamed

100 g peanut butter (crunchy or smooth)

1 tin (400 g) chopped tomatoes in juice

1 tsp cinnamon

1 tbsp ground cumin

1 tsp chilli powder

2 tsp paprika

2 tsp brown sugar

pinch of salt

2 tbsp lemon juice

fresh coriander for serving (optional)

- Heat the oven to 180 °C / gas mark 4.

- Make a few slanting cuts in the fleshy parts of the chicken joints; place them in a casserole dish. Mix the remaining ingredients in a bowl and pour over the chicken.

- Cover and cook in a pre-heated oven for 1 to 1½ hours. Stir the sauce and baste the chicken joints at least once during the cooking time, and don't let it get too dry: add water if necessary.

- Serve with boiled rice. Can be garnished with sprigs of coriander.

Note: The garlic and cinnamon can be left out if you do not like these flavours.

Nonna's Tuscan Bean Soup

from Jean Cozens

My daughter's grandmother (my ex-mother-in-law!) comes from Lucca in Tuscany and is a brilliant cook. This is real comfort food, perfect for a cold winter's evening. It's also cheap, filling and very good for you. Kidney beans are a useful source of iron, and the cheap ones in supermarkets are just as good as the more attractively packaged ones. This soup would count as two helpings of your five a day if, like me, you have seconds...

(serves 4)

2 rashers of bacon or pancetta

1 onion

1 carrot

2 sticks of celery

1 tin kidney beans

1 tin chopped tomatoes

750 ml chicken or vegetable stock (fresh, or made with 1 stock cube)

2 cloves of garlic

2 sprigs of thyme

parsley

handful of tiny pasta shapes

- Finely chop the onion, bacon, carrot and celery. Fry gently in a large pan in a little olive oil.

- Drain and rinse the kidney beans and add to the pan.

- Add the chopped tomatoes, crushed garlic, thyme and stock. Bring to the boil, cover and simmer for about half an hour.

- Take 2 ladlefuls of the soup and liquidise in a blender, then return the blended mush to the pan and stir in with a handful of chopped parsley.

- Add the pasta and cook for about 10 minutes.

- Serve with a spoonful of grated parmesan on top.

Note: If you don't eat meat, simply leave out the bacon: it will be just as good!

Caring

Grace Liggins of the Alzheimer's Society

I love the feeling of looking after my family by offering them food. I want them to feel wanted, content, cared for. I want them to come and visit me more often as a result! Maybe I'm always trying to create a 'home', whatever that really means, and a sense of warmth and comfort. My perfect evening involves family, friends, a big wooden table, a big pot of veggie curry and lots of laughter. Maybe I'm too sensible, too mumsy, but I don't mind.

Butternut Squash and Butter Bean Soup

from Michelle Baharier

This is a really simple recipe which I made up myself: I love it! It's a nourishing winter warmer and not expensive.

(serves 2–3)

vegetable oil

2 cloves of garlic, diced or crushed

1 medium Spanish onion

pinch of coriander powder

pinch of cayenne pepper (optional)

1 tbsp rice flour

1 medium butternut squash, peeled and diced

1 tin butter beans, drained and rinsed

sprig of fresh coriander leaves to garnish

- Put a little vegetable oil in a pan and sauté the onion and garlic over a low heat with the coriander powder and cayenne pepper. Don't let them brown – just soften them.

- Add a pinch of salt and the rice flour and stir till thick and dry like a dry biscuit mix.

- Add a ¼ cup of water and stir it in until the mixture thickens up, then add a further ¼ cup.

- Add the butternut squash and enough water to cover the vegetables. Let the soup boil and then turn down to a simmer. It should take around 20 minutes for the squash to cook through in an ordinary pan and 10 minutes in a pressure cooker.

- Once the butternut squash is soft, use a hand blender to liquidise the soup. If you don't have a blender, you can use a potato masher.

- Then add the butter beans and simmer covered with a lid until they're heated through.

- Serve it in bowls, garnished with chopped fresh coriander leaves on top.

Note: Tinned beans are easy to use, but to avoid added sugar and salt you can buy dried butter beans, soak them overnight, and then boil till soft.

Shepherd's Bush Pie

from Summer Farrell

Shepherd's pie is so easy to make and it reminds me of being in the cold and dark London winter and having a good hot hearty meal with the warmth of a fire, red wine and friends to brighten your spirits. It's a classic English feel-good meal, and I like to call it Shepherd's Bush Pie because that's where I live.

(serves 4)

2 tbsp olive oil

sea salt and freshly ground black pepper

500 g minced lean lamb

1 large onion, finely grated

1 large carrot, finely grated

2 cloves of garlic, finely chopped

1–2 tbsp Worcestershire sauce

1 tbsp tomato purée

handful of thyme sprigs, leaves picked

sprig of rosemary, needles chopped

250 ml red wine

300 ml chicken stock

1 kg Desiree potatoes, peeled and cut into chunks

50 g butter

2 egg yolks

parmesan, for grating

- Pre-heat the oven to 180 °C / gas mark 4.

- Heat the oil in a large pan, then season the mince and fry over a moderate to high heat for 2–3 minutes.

- Stir in the onion, carrot and garlic. Add the Worcestershire sauce, tomato purée and herbs and cook for 1–2 minutes, stirring constantly.

- Pour in the red wine and reduce until almost completely evaporated. Add the chicken stock, bring to the boil and simmer until the sauce has thickened.

- Meanwhile, cook the potatoes in boiling salted water until tender. Drain, then return to the hot pan over a low heat to dry out briefly. Pass them through a potato ricer, or just mash them, then beat in the egg yolks and butter, followed by about 2 tablespoons of grated parmesan. Season to taste.

- Spoon the mince into the bottom of a large ovenproof dish. Using a large spoon, layer the mashed potato generously on top of the mince, starting from the outside and working your way into the middle. Grate some extra parmesan over and season. Fluff up the mashed potato with a fork to make rough peaks.

- Bake in the oven for approximately 20 minutes, until bubbling and golden brown.

What do you cook to make yourself or someone else feel better?

"Some special and rare food."

"Roast chicken. Spinach soup. Macaroni and cheese. Grilled cheese sandwiches with tomato soup."

"Fish finger sandwiches with ketchup and mayo and black pepper, or spicy prawn or chicken pho with heaps of vegetables in and lots of fresh chilli and lime."

"Depends on the person and their specific psychological need. Anything from, say, chicken soup, a good goulash, fancy pasta or home-made ice cream with red fruits."

Chickpea Curry

Chickpeas and other pulses are recommended as a useful part of a diet to reduce cholesterol (thus reducing the risk of heart disease and stroke). They provide fibre and B vitamins, and some iron. And they taste delicious!

(serves 2)

3 tomatoes, chopped

½ a red or yellow pimiento or bell pepper

½ an onion, chopped

1 clove of garlic, crushed

a ½-inch piece of shredded root ginger (or ½ tbsp powdered ginger)

1 tbsp olive oil

1 tin chickpeas

pinch of ground coriander

pinch of garam masala (optional)

lemon juice

pinch of chilli powder or hot paprika

- Purée the tomatoes, pepper, onion, garlic and fresh ginger until smooth.
- Warm the oil and cook these ingredients gently, stirring from time to time.
- Add the spices and chickpeas and heat through.
- Squeeze on some lemon juice and season to taste with chilli or paprika.
- Serve with rice or couscous.

Note: A squeeze of lemon juice brings out the taste of many savoury dishes and vegetables, so it can be used in place of added salt.

Ultra-Binch

from Michael Weekes-Quinn

This dish comes from various parts of West Africa: one is Sierra Leone, my late parents' homeland. It usually goes by the name of Binch Akara but this is a variation my best friend and I came up with during a time of great personal loss: the passing of Marianne Mamawa Adama Pemagbi, my mother. A week had gone by and I was in a maelstrom of grief. My good friend Andrew Korn came to the rescue by inviting me over to his home for a meal, and I conceived the idea of preparing a Sierra Leonean dish in remembrance. Andrew and I had collaborated in cooking many times over the years, always adding that little extra something. When we finally sat down to eat and reminisce about my mother, the meal was truly uplifting.

(serves 4)

2 red onions, diced

1 white onion, diced

1 clove of garlic, mashed

400 g chicken or pork, diced

1 scotch bonnet pepper

1 tsp turmeric

1 tsp cumin seeds

1 tbsp chopped fresh ginger

500 g soaked and cooked black-eyed beans

2 tsp white or black pepper

½ tsp cayenne pepper

400 ml chicken stock or water

1 Maggi seasoning cube or a generous dash of liquid Maggi (recommended)

small bunch of freshly chopped coriander leaves

2–4 tbsp palm oil

- Dice the onions and fry in olive oil until lightly browned.

- Add the garlic and let this simmer in the oil a minute, then add the meat and brown it.

- Add the scotch bonnet pepper, turmeric, cumin and ginger, stir and seal these flavours into the meat at a high temperature.

- Add the black-eyed beans, the pepper, cayenne, stock and seasoning, and simmer for 35–45 minutes to reduce the liquid.

- Then add the coriander and palm oil and simmer for 10 more minutes.

- Serve with basmati rice or bread.

Note: 150 g (roughly 1 cup) of dried black-eyed beans should produce around 500 g cooked weight. It's also fine to use tinned black-eyed beans if you prefer. If you are using the dried ones (which is a cheaper option), soak them overnight in cold water, then rinse, bring to the boil in fresh water and simmer for 60 minutes or until just soft – remember they will be cooked further as part of the recipe.

Cheese on Toast

Steven Hampson

What I like about this food is it's very easy to make and it can be prepared very quickly. There are no set rules and you can use any quantity of ingredients you like, depending on how hungry you are. You can use any kind of cheese and bread, with margarine or butter. Over the years I must have tried many cheeses from many counties and countries: some were much enjoyed while others are best not talked about. My own personal favourite is Somerset cheese with brown bread and butter.

After I toast the bread and spread the butter I usually grill the cheese on top, but if I'm in a hurry I may melt the cheese in the microwave. Cheese on toast is a comfort food and something I've eaten for many years.

A lot of countries around the world have bread, cheese and butter, but cheese on toast is probably a European variant. When I consume this food I guess I'm partaking in something with millions of others around Europe. I will never meet the vast majority of these people but when we eat cheese on toast we share similarities and our lifestyles tally momentarily.

A Wonderful Nourishing Salad

from Michelle Baharier

(serves 2–3)

½–1 cos lettuce

1 bunch of spinach

1 bunch of rocket

4 medium sized tomatoes

½ a cucumber

1 small onion

1 red, green, yellow or orange pepper

some diced red cabbage

olives of your choice

1 tin of kidney beans

small bunch of fresh parsley

bunch of fresh basil

roasted almond flakes for topping

For the dressing:

1 tsp grainy mustard

120 ml olive oil (half a small glass)

juice of ½ a lemon

2 cloves of garlic, crushed

- Dice all the vegetables, choosing quantities according to taste. Tear up the basil leaves and chop the parsley and mix it all together.

- For the dressing, shake the garlic, mustard, lemon juice and olive oil together in a jar.

- Dress the salad, then top with the roasted almond flakes (you can roast raw almonds in the oven).

Notes: Basil and parsley can be grown on a window sill and are easy for a novice.

If you cook dried kidney beans rather than using tinned beans, they must be boiled hard for at least 10 minutes, in addition to the soaking and overall simmering they require.

Unhappy early on,
I'm later not so bad.
Perhaps the Devil's gone?
Whatever, I am glad.
I'm in a better mood
and can enjoy my food.

Peter Cox

Stir-Fried Green Beans Quickie

from Sasha Dee

(serves 2)

125 g frozen sliced green beans

125 g frozen peas

2 tbsp vegetable oil

small pinch each of methi seeds, cumin seeds and coriander seeds

1 clove of garlic, crushed

1 medium onion, finely chopped

1 bay leaf, fresh if possible

2 small to medium sized new potatoes, very finely sliced

2 small tomatoes, sliced

1 tbsp tomato purée

2 tbsp tinned chopped tomatoes, with juice

salt and pepper

brown sugar

- Thaw the peas and beans (separately) for a minute in boiling water.

- Put an empty shallow pan over a high heat for a minute. Then pour in the vegetable oil. Put in all the spices. They will pop and jump in the pan, releasing their smells and flavours. Add the crushed garlic, and when it is brown add the chopped onion and brown while turning frequently.

- Add the sliced beans and the bay leaf, and fry and stir for 2 minutes, then add the potato slices and stir for another 2 minutes.

- Put in all the tomato ingredients; mix well. Sprinkle a spoonful of water over and cover the pan for 4 minutes. Then check with a fork that the potato is cooked.

- Finally add the green peas and leave the pan covered but off the heat for a minute so that they can heat through.

- Season to taste and, if your tomatoes are very acidic, add a very small amount of brown sugar to balance the flavour.

- Eat with toast, naan or pitta bread, or just as it is.

Strange Dish

Sasha Dee, trustee at CoolTan Arts

Whenever I saw my old college friend, we eventually went to have a meal. He was tremendously enthusiastic and bubbly when talk came around to fish or seafood – or just food! He would always mention his favourite dish that his mother used to cook – that is, black bean curry made with freshly ground spices and herbs and diced fresh coconut, served on boiled rice, along with tiny fish like sprats freshly fried with coarsely pounded coriander seeds, peppercorns, pressed green ginger and a touch of garlic. I never ate this dish because he never cooked it, but I always enjoyed the way he talked about it – as if he had eaten it just a few minutes ago. Perhaps the dish was not real, but a figment of his imagination. Anyway, he derived a lot of pleasure from talking about it.

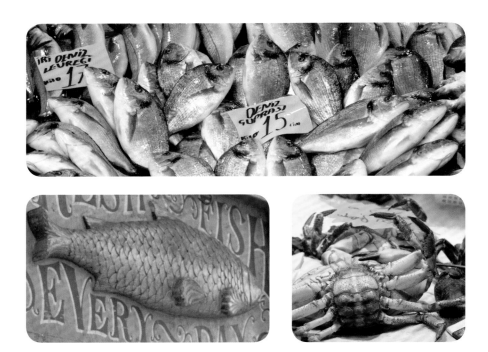

Seafood Medley in Spiced Coconut Milk

from Sasha Dee

(serves 4)

200 g each of 2 or 3 kinds of fish, boned and cut into 4-inch pieces

200 g other seafood (e.g. mussels, prawns, clams)

1 tin good coconut milk

1 tsp turmeric powder

1 tsp curry powder

1 tsp cumin powder

1 tsp chilli powder

1 cinnamon stick

1 bay leaf

1 cardamom pod

½ a Spanish onion, cut into rings

a few cloves of garlic, peeled and crushed

juice of ½ a lemon

a little pinch of brown sugar

sea salt and pepper

- In a large saucepan, bring the coconut milk to a gentle simmer. Add the cardamom pod, cinnamon stick, bay leaf and all the other spices. Keep the heat low and stir well to make sure it doesn't curdle.

- In a flat pan, heat a spoonful of vegetable oil with a good knob of butter. When the butter has melted, gently fry the fish with the skin side uppermost, just to seal the flesh and half-cook it.

- Take the fish off the heat and put it into the coconut milk. Add the other seafood and stir gently.

- Into the same flat pan, pour some more oil. When it is heated put in the crushed garlic and the onion rings and fry them till they're golden brown. Add to the coconut fish mixture.

- Add the lemon juice and sugar, and season with salt and pepper.

- Serve on boiled rice.

Rice Noodle Salad

from Michelle Baharier

Being a veggie is one thing, but having an allergy to wheat is quite another! It means you can't eat pasta, so rice noodle salad is a dream for me. Rice noodles are relatively inexpensive as long as you buy the Chinese brands.

(serves 2)

½ a pack of rice noodles, cooked and rinsed in cold water

1 large onion, finely diced

2 large tomatoes

100 g good quality olives of your choice

4 sun-dried tomatoes, sliced

½ a medium cucumber, diced

200 g baby spinach leaves, washed and chopped

¼ of a bunch of basil, torn up

10 dates with stones out, chopped

salt and pepper

olive oil

- Prepare all the ingredients. Tear rather than chop the basil as it preserves the flavour better. Use any olives you like: I love the green ones stuffed with red peppers and mixed with lemon and garlic.

- Mix everything together, season it to taste and drizzle with olive oil.

Asian Wokery! Stir-Fried Cabbage

from Okelly Chee

You can cook the lowly white cabbage in various ways: fried in a European steel pan, baked in the oven, boiled in a soup East European-style, boiled and drained as part of soggy meat-and-two-veg English-style, pickled in vinegar Polish-style, served as sauerkraut German-style, grilled, steamed, cooked in a slow-cooker, microwaved or raw in a salad. Or it can be stir-fried in the Eastern wok. They all taste different, but the best taste is the wok-fried version – and it's healthier and strictly vegetarian!

(serves 2–4)

soy or vegetable oil

½ a cabbage, sliced

½ a stock cube

garlic or onions, sliced (optional)

soy sauce (optional)

- Put a little oil into the wok and heat it till it sizzles.

- Put in the cabbage (and garlic or onion if you are using them), and keep turning it over with a spoon or spatula while it cooks.

- Dissolve the stock cube in a tea-cup of boiling hot water. You can use any stock cube: French Knorr, English Oxo or Asian gluten. Add this sauce to the cabbage and keep frying a little longer.

- Don't cook the cabbage too long. The secret of wok-frying is to have the vegetables al dente, not over-cooked.

- You can serve this with a little bit of light, low-salt soy sauce or sweet dark soy depending on your taste.

KITCHEN ARTISTRY

To cook is to create. From the simplest snack to the finest meal, the way we put colours and flavours together shows inspiration, imagination and brilliance.

Chinese Fusion Soup

from Michelle Baharier

This is a recipe I made up. It reminds me of being a child and having chicken and sweetcorn soup from a Chinese take-away.

(serves 2)

1 large onion, sliced

110g mushrooms, sliced

1 cup frozen sweetcorn

pinch of saffron

pinch of salt

2 eggs

½–1 cup spelt flour

250g rice vermicelli noodles

- Half fill a medium sized pan with water, drop in the sliced onion, mushrooms, corn, saffron and salt, bring to the boil and then turn the heat down so it's just simmering.

- Take a tablespoonful of liquid from the soup and place it in a bowl. Crack an egg into the liquid and whisk it up with a fork.

- Add the spelt flour to the egg and make a wet dough that's solid enough to roll into small balls, about the size of walnuts. Depending on the size of your egg you may need more or less flour: the overall texture should be moist and firm, but not wet.

- Crack the other egg into the soup. Cook for a minute before using a fork to whisk it in.

- Add the vermicelli and the spelt-dough balls and cook for about 10 minutes. The balls are ready when they float to the top, and you can test the vermicelli by tasting it.

Note: You can easily leave out the spelt-dough balls. You can also leave out the egg, making it a good dish for vegans. There are various possible additions too: frozen peas, grated cheese, soy sauce or Tamari instead of the salt... Get creative!

Jean's Stuffed Cabbage

from Jean Cozens

I think this recipe originates in Central Europe – I found it in a cookbook which has since bitten the dust and I adapted it. Cabbage is not only good for you, it is also good for the planet because it is grown here in Britain. You could equally well use the rice mixture here to stuff peppers or courgettes.

(serves 2–3)

8 large cabbage leaves taken from the outside of the cabbage

1 onion, chopped

1 tin chopped tomatoes

2 cloves of garlic, chopped

thyme

100g beef, quorn or soy mince

1 cup cooked rice

100g chopped mushrooms (optional)

soy sauce

black pepper

- Heat the oven to 180°C / gas mark 4.

- To make the tomato sauce, fry half the onion gently for 10 minutes. Add the tomatoes, garlic and some thyme and cook for 20 minutes uncovered on a low heat. If you're feeling lazy or pressed for time, you can use half a carton of V8 juice instead.

- Fry the other half of the onion in a little oil. Add the mince, stir until it browns, then add the mushrooms and the rice. Beef needs to cook for longer than soy or quorn. Add a dash of soy sauce, some black pepper and a spoonful of the tomato sauce.

- Cut the thick stems off the cabbage leaves; parboil for 5–7 minutes in a large pan with plenty of water. Keep checking them: you want them bright green, not boiled to death.

- Drain the cabbage leaves and lay them on a clean work surface. Put a tablespoonful of rice mixture in the centre of each one and roll it up into a cigar shape.

- Lay them side by side in an oven dish, pour over the sauce, cover with foil and bake in the oven for half an hour.

Fish and Courgette Ribbon Salad

from Pablo Antoli

This is a really quick, low-fat salad. It's great on its own as a healthy light lunch, and it looks quite beautiful on the plate.

(serves 2)

250g cooked fish (e.g. sea bass, tuna, mackerel)

2 large courgettes

4 tomatoes, cut into wedges

For the dressing:

1 tbsp lemon juice

1 tbsp Dijon mustard

4 tbsp extra virgin olive oil

1 tsp soy sauce

1 clove of garlic, crushed

2 tbsp capers

black pepper

- Wash the courgettes, then top and tail. Use a vegetable peeler to slice them into long thin ribbons. Place these into a shallow serving dish, salt the ribbons and let them sit for about 30 minutes to an hour, then rinse, squeeze out the excess liquid, and pat dry.

- To make the dressing, whisk together the lemon juice, mustard, olive oil and soy sauce, then add the crushed garlic and capers, and season to taste with pepper.

- Place the courgette ribbons on a plate with the tomatoes and big chunks of fish.

- Dress the salad with the caper dressing.

Cheesy-Hammy-Eggy Topside

Cooking creatively doesn't have to mean complex cooking: just combining tastes in new and delicious ways is kitchen artistry... and toast is the perfect carrier for all sorts of things! This is a quick and tasty lunch.

(serves 1)

bread

ham

cheese

egg

- Toast a slice of bread.
- Put a slice of ham on the toast, and cover the ham with thinly sliced cheese. Place under the grill until the cheese has melted.
- While it is under the grill, fry or poach an egg.
- Place the cooked egg on top of the cheese... and enjoy!

Note: You can add to these basic ingredients of course: try mustard or pickle, tomatoes, spinach, even (Central European-style) thinly sliced apple.

Leftovers

If you have leftover potatoes, rice or vegetables you can turn them into something new just by adding grated cheese or tomato sauce. Cold boiled potatoes can be sliced up and used in a Spanish omelette: fry some garlic and onions if you have them, add the potato slices or any other omelette-friendly leftovers and pour beaten egg over the top. Then cook very slowly, finishing the top side under the grill if necessary. Leftovers are always good to go into a soup, and extra boiled rice can be added at the last minute to a lovely crisp, fresh vegetable stir fry – just make sure it heats through thoroughly.

What's your best cooking skill?

"Basic homey stuff – nothing fancy, but relatively nourishing comfort food. And I like baking bread."

"Planning ahead. Doing more than needed and loving leftovers."

"Baking. Dumplings."

"Cooking for a small group, I like to try gourmet dishes. For a large group, I make easy dishes like curry, rice and some sweets."

"The truth is I never follow recipes – I get inspired by food. Like if I'm out cycling, I might see something on a restaurant menu, and then I'll cook it. But I wouldn't Google it – I'll just buy the ingredients and cook it."

One-Pot Cooking

from Anna Cochrane

One-pot cooking isn't just about avoiding the washing up. You can make a quick and easy dish when you need it or you can let flavours simmer together over time, so it's perfect for soups and stews. It's also great if your cooking space is limited to only one or two burners. Here are some recipes that can be made in one saucepan.

One-Pot Spicy Chicken and Noodle Soup

(serves 1)

This is a quick and easy version of Pho, the Vietnamese dish. Peel and chop a large clove of garlic and a piece of root ginger about the size of your thumbnail. Fry these with ½ tsp chilli flakes in a heavy-bottomed saucepan on a low heat. With scissors, cut a large chicken breast into small pieces into the pot and fry until evenly white. Add 350 ml water and bring to the boil. Crumble in a chicken stock cube, add 200 g frozen peas and cook until tender. In the last couple of minutes add a portion of egg noodles and stir until cooked through. You can top it with a handful of fresh coriander and a wedge of lime if you like. If you are vegetarian, you can use miso paste instead of chicken stock and either omit the chicken or substitute with tofu.

One-Pot Moroccan-Style Lamb and Chickpea Stew

(serves 4)

This is a bigger, heartier stew, good for more people, or to last you a few days. Heat 3 tbsp olive oil in a large heavy-bottomed saucepan and add ½ tsp each of cumin seeds, chilli flakes, ground cinnamon and ground ginger. Gently fry 1 onion, thickly chopped, and 3 cloves of garlic, whole. Add 650 g boned shoulder of lamb cut into large pieces and fry until evenly browned. Add a glass of red wine, 750 ml meat stock, a little salt and black pepper, and bring to the boil. Throw in 4 carrots, peeled but whole, and 2 or 3 small potatoes, peeled and halved. Simmer for at least 1 hour with the lid on, stirring occasionally and adding water if more liquid is required. Add 150 g pitted prunes and cook for another 30 minutes without the lid. Stir in a can of chickpeas, drained and rinsed, and cook for another 10 minutes. Serve with warm bread. If you don't want to use it, the wine can be omitted completely.

One-Pot Pea and Lemon Risotto

(serves 2)

This would be a nice dish to make for a guest. Finely chop 1 onion and 2 cloves of garlic. Boil the kettle and use it to make about half a litre (two mugs) of vegetable stock – keep that standing by. Gently heat 2 tbsp olive oil and a large knob of butter in a large frying pan and fry the onion and garlic with ½ tsp dried thyme until soft and translucent. Add 200g risotto rice (Arborio rice) and stir for a minute until it looks translucent. Add a little salt and pepper. Add a glass of white wine and stir until absorbed into the rice. On a low heat start to add the stock a bit at a time, letting each addition absorb into the rice before you add the next and stirring throughout. It should take about 15 minutes of slow stirring. Near the end, cook 200g of frozen peas (you can just pour boiling water over them in a mug or bowl). Check the rice is cooked (it should be al dente) and stir in the peas and the juice of a lemon. Remove from the heat and add another knob of butter and a handful of grated parmesan and stir in. Cover and let it sit for 2 minutes. Can be served alone or is also excellent with grilled fish. If you don't want to use it, the wine can be omitted completely.

Coriander Balls in Lentil Curry

from Sasha Dee

This is like tarka dahl (an Indian spiced lentil recipe), but with the addition of coriander-flavoured balls a bit like spicy dumplings, which turn it into something really special.

(serves 2–3)

For the lentil curry:
1 cup lentils, any variety
1 tbsp brown sugar
¼ tbsp tamarind paste
1 tsp turmeric
1 tsp curry powder
¼ tsp chilli powder

For the tarka spice mixture:
1 tbsp turmeric
1 tbsp garam masala
1 tbsp curry powder
1 inch of cinnamon bark
2 cardamom pods
pinch each of methi seeds, coriander seeds and peppercorns

For the coriander balls:
½ cup gram flour
½ cup rice flour or corn flour
handful of coriander leaves, finely chopped
½ tsp cumin powder
½ tsp curry powder
a few leaves of fresh basil, coarsely chopped
pinch each of rosemary, marjoram, dill
1 cup boiled moong dal (mung beans)
a few small spinach leaves
1 clove of garlic, crushed
2 medium onions, finely chopped

- Put the lentils into a saucepan that's a quarter full of boiling water, and place over a high heat. Add the rest of the curry ingredients, cover and simmer, keeping an eye on it and adding a little water every so often to make sure the water level stays just above the lentils.

- While this is cooking, make the coriander balls. Put the gram flour and rice (or corn) flour into a bowl. Add the herbs and spices and season lightly with salt and pepper. Mix well and then stir in the moong dal, spinach, garlic and onions.

- Mix well with your fingers and the palm of your hand, adding water little by little until the mixture is like dough. Taste a little bit of the mixture to check the balance of flavours, then form it into small balls about the size of ping-pong balls.

- Heat a couple of spoonfuls of vegetable oil in a shallow pan. Gently fry the balls just to seal them all around. Do not deep fry. When done, take them out of the pan and leave to drain on kitchen paper.

- Once the lentils are cooked, add the coriander balls and turn the heat down.

- Finally, make the tarka. Put 2 tablespoons of vegetable oil in the pan used for sealing the coriander balls, and place it over a high heat. Put in all the tarka spices, and when they are jumping in the oil lift the pan off the heat and pour the spicy oil onto the hot curry.

- Serve it with raita or plain yoghurt, accompanied by rice or naan bread if you like.

Note: For the lentil curry you can use any variety of lentils – or a mixture of two different types. Red lentils cook the most quickly.

Mooli Raita

from Sasha Dee

This dish is a side dish, good to serve with many types of hot dishes, especially spicy ones. Mooli and yoghurt are a nice way to change the taste in the mouth, and also good for the stomach. Moolis are white radishes and come mainly from the Indian sub-continent, though they can be found as far afield as Kenya, the Caribbean islands, and China. The word mooli is Sanskrit in origin and means root.

(serves 4)

1 mooli (or ½ a long one)

small carton of plain yoghurt

pinch each of cumin powder, cumin seeds, coriander powder, chilli powder

a few sprigs of fresh coriander, finely chopped

a few spring onions, finely chopped

½ tbsp olive oil

- Wash the mooli and grate it roughly.

- Pour the yoghurt into a bowl and mix in the grated mooli, all the spices one by one, and lastly the oil. Mix well and leave in the fridge a while to allow the flavours to blend.

- Serve chilled, garnished with the chopped spring onion and coriander.

Turmeric Raita

Fresh turmeric can be found in Indian shops and sometimes even ordinary super-markets. It has a very particular taste, somewhat different from the powder, and it would be enough just to add some grated fresh turmeric to yoghurt to make a delicious raita, but if you want to add more flavours, you can. So, for example, to a large carton of yoghurt try adding a 1-inch piece of fresh turmeric, grated, a little chopped fresh ginger and a 1-inch green chilli, also finely chopped, along with some chopped fresh spinach and coriander leaves, and a little bit of grated nutmeg. Blend the ingredients well and then leave to chill for a while before serving.

Salmon Pasta in Cucumber Cream Sauce

from Kathrin Kirrmann

A friend of mine cooked this recipe when I was volunteering in Belfast. It always reminds me of the 2 months I lived in Belfast, and my fellow volunteers there. It's a bit unusual with the cooked cucumbers, but very tasty, and it gives you lots of energy and vitamins. My parents loved the meal when I cooked it for them. It's fairly easy and quick to cook, and not very expensive if you use frozen or smoked salmon. I love it!

(serves 4)

2 cucumbers

1–2 tbsp vegetable oil

2 tbsp flour

½–1 cup vegetable stock

200 ml single cream

2–3 tbsp wholegrain mustard

200–300 g salmon (or other fish – fresh, smoked or frozen)

fresh lemon juice

500 g pasta

- Peel the 2 cucumbers, cut them in half lengthways, deseed, and slice into 1 cm-thick pieces.

- Cut the salmon into bite-size pieces.

- Put the cucumbers into a cooking pan with the oil and sprinkle the flour over them. Add the vegetable stock (use boiling water and part of a vegetable stock cube) and the cream.

- Bring everything to the boil and then simmer on a low temperature for 10 minutes.

- Add the wholegrain mustard, the salmon and the lemon juice if you want that.

- Simmer over a low heat for 5 more minutes.

- Serve this sauce with any kind of pasta.

Colourful Colcannon

from Kevin Fleisch

I'm a quarter Irish, and colcannon is a great Irish dish which can be eaten in many variations, either on its own or used as the carbohydrate/veg part of your meal with a meat dish. It's great as leftovers: if you want you can re-heat it and then put cheese on top and grill it, or half-cook an omelette (cheese or plain) then mix it into the pre-heated colcannon.

Quantities of individual ingredients can be varied – feel free to experiment – but potato should be the majority vegetable, and about 1 kilo of vegetables in total will feed 4 people.

turnip or swede, diced

potatoes, diced

sweet potatoes, diced

cabbage – red and green, chopped

leeks, sliced

onions, chopped

peppers, chopped

splash of milk

knob of butter

- Put a pan of water on to boil while you chop up all the vegetables. I peel the turnips, but just wash or scrub the potatoes and sweet potatoes and leave their fibre-rich skins on.

- Get the turnips or swedes into the water first, and boil them for about 10 minutes while you carry on chopping the rest.

- Add the diced potatoes and/or sweet potatoes to the pan, then after another 10 minutes add cabbage, leeks, onions, and multi-coloured peppers.

- About 10 minutes later (30 minutes total cooking time), strain the mix, saving the water for soup or stock.

- Add your version of milk and butter (vegetarian options are fine) and mash. It's a rough mash – not a smoothie – with lots of different colours and textures.

Knowing Your Lettuce

Ari Henry

Let's go wild and cook a salad: it's easy, nourishing and cheap!

It's not unusual for people to feel put off this kind of cookery that doesn't need cooking: many people only ever see salad ingredients ready prepared in polythene bags, or sitting on a plate, or in a sandwich. But let's leave these behind and try a grocer... Remember, they don't bite: they want your money. Ask for a lettuce if that's what you want to do; in the few small greengrocers' left, they'll probably come with you to the spot. Here it gets awkward: which lettuce? "That one's got red bits!" Relax. Lettuces are all lettuces at the end of the day, and here's where the fun begins: you just pick which type of lettuce you like the look of. Next time you go you can pick a different one. The lettuce can be used as a garnish (to make the food look pretty) or you can use it as a wrap, allowing you to pick up food without using cutlery. Once you are confident at the grocer's, add another salad item, possibly tomatoes. Eating a tomato will stop hunger pangs as well as a chocolate bar can, and is far healthier.

Salad

Salads can be pretty much anything you want them to be. They can include both raw and cooked ingredients, and can be made from vegetables alone or bulked up with rice, couscous, lentils, chickpeas, nuts or nuggets of cheese. That makes them a terrific way of using whatever you have in the fridge or can find in the market, and also means you need never get bored: the more you experiment, the more possibilities you will find.

There are salad recipes throughout this book, but here's a collection of simple salads that work well in combination with each other, or with other bits of food, and could all become part of your regular eating habits. Needless to say, you can adapt them all to your own taste or budget very easily.

Roasted Peppers

These are very tasty served with pita bread alongside baba ghanoush, some green leaves and any kind of yoghurt dip. You can use any kind of pepper: red, green, orange or yellow, or a mixture of all of them. They also keep in the fridge for a few days.

Just wash the peppers and chop them into strips, which you then place under a hot grill until the skin starts to blacken. Bring them out and let them cool (some people swear by placing them in a paper bag for this stage), then peel off the blackened skin. These are much tastier than the roasted peppers sold in jars, which can have lots of preservatives in them, and much cheaper too, if you buy your peppers from a local market.

Uncle Frank's Salad

¼ of a raw cauliflower, broken into florets

10 baby tomatoes

½ a cucumber

½ a lettuce

handful of flat leaf parsley

- Chop up all the ingredients, toss them together and add your own dressing.

Cucumber with Dill

1 large cucumber, very thinly sliced

1 medium onion, very thinly sliced

white wine vinegar or cider vinegar

handful of fresh dill, chopped

- Lay the cucumber slices out on a tea towel and pat to remove a bit of the moisture.

- Place them in a bowl with the slivers of onion and a pinch of salt and stir well, then leave to stand for 10 minutes or so.

- Add a light sprinkle of vinegar and the dill, stir and leave to chill in the fridge for 1 or 2 hours before eating.

Coleslaw

Home-made coleslaw is something totally different from the shop-bought stuff.

½ a medium cabbage, either white or red, or a bit of each for colour

2–3 carrots, shredded or grated

1 large onion, diced

mayonnaise (dairy or vegan)

- Slice the raw vegetables as finely as you can, by hand or in a food processor (if you don't already have one, treat yourself and never look back!).

- Mix the vegetables together in a large bowl with just enough mayonnaise to bind them, and season lightly with salt and pepper.

Notes: The Romans used cabbages as medicine for centuries. Recent cancer research suggests that it may indeed help prevent the disease.

You can experiment with the ingredients, adding apples, walnuts or raisins to the basic mix. You can also substitute plain yoghurt for the mayonnaise.

Greek/Turkish Salad

½ a pack of feta cheese, cubed or crumbled

4 large tomatoes, diced

½ a cucumber, diced

¼ of a lettuce – use any kind you like, or a mixture of leaves

2 carrots, grated

100 g black olives

lemon juice

olive oil

* Just get a bowl, chop your ingredients up and mix them all together, then add olive oil and lemon juice to taste.

Dips and Dressings for Salads

Ready-made salad dressings seem convenient, but they're actually very expensive compared to making dressings yourself, and often quite sugary. Here are some ideas for things you can easily make at home. Many will serve as either dips or salad dressings. If you're getting together with friends, a bowl of olives and a selection of dips is delicious, and can look very bright and colourful too: serve them with sticks of raw carrot, celery and cucumber.

Mustard Vinaigrette

Put a teaspoonful of wholegrain mustard in a glass and stir in 1–2 inches of olive oil. Add 2–3 cloves of garlic, crushed or finely chopped, and stir well. Then add the juice from a quarter or half of a lemon, or vinegar instead (you can use any white, red wine or cider vinegar, but not malt). Judge the balance by taste, though the general rule of thumb is 1 part lemon juice or vinegar to 3 parts oil. You can vary this recipe by adding torn basil leaves, thyme, or any other green herb that you like. You can also give the dressing a different character by adding a little tamari or soy sauce along with the vinegar, or a pinch of curry powder instead of the mustard.

Thousand Island Dressing

Add paprika (or Tabasco or other chilli sauce) to mayonnaise and you've got Thousand Island without the junk! You can also add some ketchup or tomato purée for a pinker colour, and Worcestershire sauce gives it a little kick. This is tasty with salads or sandwiches, or even as a dip.

Coronation Sauce

Add turmeric and curry powder to mayonnaise and you get another tasty dressing – this time bright yellow. Good with salads made of crunchy foods like celery, apple, fennel, kohlrabi and chicory.

Yoghurt Dips

Blend a bunch of coriander with half a litre of yoghurt in a liquidiser: this has a wonderful flavour and is an amazing green colour. Or mix finely diced cumber and mint leaves into yoghurt, with lemon juice and garlic if you like. Many cuisines feature a variation of this cool and refreshing dip.

Food Growing Projects

Maggie Jay

By eating foods that are raw or freshly sprouted we can often optimise their nutritional value. This increasingly popular method of food preparation assists in strengthening the immune system and bringing incredible vitality to the body.

Growing your own food is a great way to get access to raw foods, and luckily, in Southwark, food growing communities are sprouting up all over the place – particularly in the allotments along the route of the old Surrey Canal.

Here, local groups such as Transition Town Peckham harvest an abundance of clean, beautiful, naturally grown vegetables, including courgettes, beans and carrots, which are great for you, and have a very low carbon footprint, contributing to the health of the planet as well.

At the Burgess Park Food Project, a group of local people share their skills and experience to promote organic horticulture, permaculture, and an understanding of the value of healthy, local, fresh food. Drawing the local community together, they are also improving the green environment, and bringing a boost of positive energy to the life of the park.

These groups are expanding, and they welcome volunteers at all times of the year. Even if you don't have a balcony or a back garden of your own, you can join a food growing community and green up the earth!

FEAST DAYS

We use food to celebrate and to mark significant occasions. For cultural, religious or just personal reasons, there's always a way to make a meal special.

Moroccan Couscous

from Abdellah Smita

In Morocco, family meals maintain family unity and spirit. Nowadays, as the country is changing and people are busy with their professional lives, family mealtimes are not as frequent as they used to be. However, people are trying to maintain their cultural habits and still do their best to have Friday lunch with their families.

In the UK, couscous is known as one of the fastest meals to cook. This is not true for Moroccans! In Morocco, it's a traditional dish served every Friday that requires several hours of cooking. Friday is a special day when men wear traditional djellabas, with prayers that are different from those during the week.

Couscous is usually followed by green tea with mint (see the Cup of Joy chapter).

(serves 8)

500 g couscous

salt

¼ cup sunflower or vegetable oil

2 medium onions, coarsely chopped

1 tsp coriander powder

1 tsp crushed red chillies

½ tsp saffron

1 tsp cumin powder

1 kg boneless lamb, cut into 2-inch chunks

a 1.4 kg chicken, cut into 8 pieces

500 g carrots, peeled and cut into 1-inch chunks

2 green peppers, cut into ½-inch strips

500 g tomatoes, cut into large wedges

500 g yellow or butternut squash, peeled and cut into slices 1 inch by 2 inches

350 g string beans (fresh or frozen) or peas

1 tin chickpeas, drained

225 g black raisins

fresh parsley

- Put the couscous into a large bowl with a cup of cold water and 1 tablespoon of salt. Stir it up with a fork and allow it to stand for 10 minutes to swell.

- Spread the couscous out in a colander lined with cheese cloth (or in the top of a couscousière – see note). Place the colander over a pan which is half filled with simmering water, on a low heat. Cover with foil and let steam for 10 minutes.

- In a large saucepan (or the bottom part of your couscousière), sauté the onions in the oil until soft, along with 1 teaspoon of salt plus the spices.

- Add the lamb and 2 litres of water. Then fit the colander with the couscous in it over the meat, cover with foil, and allow everything to simmer gently for 30 minutes.

- Add the chicken pieces to the stew and continue cooking for 30 minutes, stirring the couscous occasionally to separate the grains.

- Add to the stew the vegetables, chickpeas and raisins, taste for seasoning, and then cook for about 15 minutes or until the vegetables are tender but still slightly crisp.

- Tip the couscous into a large serving bowl or platter, make a large hole in the centre, and arrange the meat and vegetables attractively within, pouring the cooking liquid, which is your sauce, over it all.

- Garnish with sprigs of parsley.

Note: A couscousière is a large double boiler with holes in the bottom of the upper pot that allow its contents to steam. You can improvise your own couscousière using a large pot and a metal colander lined with cheese cloth, with a piece of heavy-duty foil as a tight lid.

Zighini – a Spicy Eritrean Stew

from Stella Camugino

Zighini is a recipe typical of my country, Eritrea, and is cooked on special occasions. It's a meat and chilli stew, and is very spicy, but you can use less berbere and still enjoy the real taste of this delicious East African dish. Whenever I make zighini it brings back memories of my childhood in Eritrea, and since I haven't been there for the last 12 years it gives me a nostalgic feeling.

(serves 4)

3 tbsp oil

2 large onions, finely chopped

750 ml water

3 tbsp clarified butter

1–3 tbsp berbere (Eritrean/Ethiopian spice mixture)

225 g tinned chopped tomatoes

300 g beef, lamb or chicken, cut into bite-sized chunks

a 1-inch piece of ginger, finely chopped

2 large cloves of garlic, finely chopped

4 boiled eggs

3 or more injera (see note)

- Fry the onions in the oil over a very low heat, stirring, until softened. Add a cup of water, the clarified butter and the berbere. Cook for a few minutes, stirring.

- When the mixture has become a paste, add the tomatoes. Simmer for 10 minutes, stirring occasionally, then add a cup of water and the meat. Cook until much of the sauce is absorbed, then add another cup of water and leave to simmer.

- While the meat is cooking, boil some eggs, drain and peel them.

- When the meat is softened, add the ginger, garlic and whole boiled eggs, and leave to cook for 10 minutes.

- You eat this dish with your hands, using torn-off pieces of injera to scoop up the sauce.

Note: Injera is a spongy flatbread like a pancake, traditionally made from teff flour. Staffordshire oatcakes could make a good, untraditional replacement!

Matzo Ball Soup

Matzo (or matzah) is a hard, cracker-like bread made from a dough which has not been allowed to rise. Jewish people eat matzo at Pesach, to remember how quickly the Israelites left Egypt. Matzo meal, made from crumbled matzo, is similar to breadcrumbs. It can be used to make dumplings that go perfectly into either chicken or vegetable broth.

(serves 8)

4 eggs, lightly beaten

4 tbsp vegetable oil

salt and pepper

2–3 litres prepared chicken or vegetable stock

4 egg whites, beaten to soft peaks

170 ml (¾ cup) matzo meal

2 tbsp grated onion or finely chopped spring onions (optional)

1 carrot, thinly sliced

a few sprigs of dill (optional)

- Beat together the eggs and oil with a scant teaspoon of salt and a dash of pepper until creamy. Mix in 4 tablespoons of stock and then fold this mixture into the beaten egg whites (the egg whites are optional, but they make the balls nice and light).

- Gradually fold the matzo meal into the egg mixture, then chill for 1 hour. During this time the matzo meal absorbs the liquid and becomes soft.

- Remove from fridge, mix in the onion (if using), then moisten your hands and shape the batter into ½-inch balls (the quantities above make about 24 balls).

- Bring your stock to the boil and drop the dumplings in one by one, then cover the pan and simmer for 30 minutes. 10 minutes before the end, add the sliced carrot.

- Ladle some soup and a couple of matzo balls into each bowl and top with dill sprigs.

Note: To make fresh vegetable stock, simply sweat some onion and carrots in a little olive oil for 3–5 minutes, with other vegetables like leek, celery or fennel if you like. Cover this with cold water and add flavours such as garlic, peppercorns, bay leaves and other green herbs, bring to the boil and simmer for 15–20 minutes. Then strain the liquid to remove all the vegetable and herb pieces, and you are left with vegetable stock. Delicious!

Pesach Dinner

Asia Wieloch

At CoolTan Arts, we like to find reasons to share food together! One celebration feast we have had here was a Pesach dinner. We wanted to introduce this important Jewish holiday, firstly to celebrate the rich cultural diversity of the borough we live in, and secondly because we thought the idea behind Pesach could hold significance for everyone. Pesach commemorates the story of the Exodus, in which the ancient Israelites were freed from slavery in Egypt. Each of us has our own story which, on a personal level, carries a meaning similar to the end of slavery. It could be dealing with our mental health distress, or going through a particularly difficult period in life. Symbolic foods are eaten at Pesach, from the seder plate, and the evening is filled telling stories about the Exodus. At our Pesach dinner everyone got involved in the process while eating some delicious food.

Charoset

from Michelle Baharier

Pesach was the most important festival of my childhood. It takes place at home with guests and friends, and it's a major family event. We would sing songs and celebrate our history and culture. Charoset is one of the symbolic foods eaten just once a year at the Pesach table. It looks a bit like pinkish mud, but it is meant to represent the mortar which the Israelite slaves used in their buildings in Egypt – and it does taste good!

(serves 6)

6 apples, peeled, cored and chopped

½ cup finely chopped walnuts

½ cup unsalted shelled pistachio nuts (not dyed red), toasted

½ cup whole almonds, toasted

1 tsp white sugar

3½ tsp honey

80 ml kosher sweet red wine

1–2 tsp ground cinnamon

1 tsp ground allspice

1 tsp ground nutmeg

1 tsp ground cloves

- Roughly chop the nuts and apples.

- Place all the ingredients into a food processor and mix to a paste.

Roots of Happiness

from Sasha Dee

This dish is light on the stomach, but filling when one is very hungry. In markets like those in Brixton, East Street and Lewisham, root vegetables are very cheap. One can use as many types as one likes, but no one vegetable should dominate the overall taste, which should be a medley of all the ingredients blended together. Note that root vegetables have different cooking times (potatoes the longest). They should not be over-cooked. This will probably take a couple of hours to prepare and cook, so give yourself plenty of time, and enjoy the process.

(serves 10)

Root vegetables:

1 sweet potato, 4–5 medium-sized old potatoes, 1 baking potato

2 beetroots, 4 carrots, 4 parsnips, 2 cassava, 200 g yam

1 mooli (a long Indian radish root, also called daikon)

Green herbs:

pinch each of basil, dill, fennel, marjoram, rosemary, sage

1 bay leaf

Spices:

pinch each of methi seeds, coriander seeds, peppercorns

1 inch of cinnamon bark, 1 piece of star anise, 2 cardamom pods

1 tbsp each of turmeric powder, garam masala and curry powder

Complementary flavours:

6 inches of leek, sliced

2 big spoonfuls of each of two types of lentils (e.g. red lentils, moong dal)

1 cup dried chickpeas, soaked overnight (or at least 8 hours)

1 small whole bulb of garlic, minced

1 large onion, diced

1 tbsp tomato purée, 2 chopped fresh tomatoes, and 1 tin chopped tomatoes

4 inch-long green chillies, finely chopped

a ½-inch piece of root ginger

250 g diced butternut squash and 250 g diced pumpkin

4 slices of pineapple, a few grapes, 1 sweet and 1 cooking apple, both diced

1 fresh mango

handful of spinach leaves, 250 g frozen peas

1 tbsp honey and a pinch of brown sugar

a few sprigs of coriander for serving

- Boil a kettle full of water and keep it hot for use throughout cooking. Dice the root vegetables into big cubes; cut the pumpkin and squash a bit smaller.

- Place a large, deep saucepan a quarter full of boiling water over a medium heat. Put in the hardest roots (like potatoes), with the two varieties of lentils and the leek for flavour, cover and simmer. When they are part-cooked (after 4–5 minutes), add the other root vegetables and the green herbs and boil for 2 minutes.

- Add the chickpeas and enough boiling water to cover all the vegetables, and put the lid back on. Add more boiling water as necessary to keep the roots just covered.

- In a small pan, gently heat 2 tablespoons of vegetable oil. Put in the whole dry spices and after a moment add the garlic. When that turns brown add the onion, and when this is brown, add the powdered spices and mix well.

- After 2 more minutes, add the tomato purée and mix well, then add all the tomatoes and mix. After a minute or so, add the green chillies and ginger and mix.

- Now add the spicy sauce to the roots in the main pot, along with the squash, pumpkin, pineapple, grapes and apples. Mix, add the brown sugar and honey and some water if necessary, and put the lid on.

- Peel the mango and add the whole fruit to the pot: it will be covered in sweet sticky flesh which will mix with the sauce, and the stone can be removed at the end.

- Taste, and season with salt and pepper. By now, everything should have blended to give a mix of sweet, bitter and tangy. Add sugar to balance the flavours if necessary.

- Add the spinach and peas, and just enough water so that it covers the vegetables by half an inch. Turn the heat right down and simmer 5 more minutes.

- Serve garnished with coriander, on rice, with plain or naan bread, or just on its own.

A Meal for One

from Ari Henry

The majority of human beings feel lonely at some point in their lives, particularly when living alone. Living alone can lead to sloppy habits, with food typically the microwave ready meal or fast food eaten on the bus. This recipe is designed to take away that hole of loneliness or to make a healthy evening diet more fun.

If the microwave ready meal has become a habit, it is quite acceptable to incorporate it here, as this recipe is aimed at slow change and not some magical overnight cure. Do try and go for a meal that is vaguely healthy if possible. This recipe is suitable for all homes, from the one that has everything to one with just the basic kitchen minimum.

(serves 1)

1 bunch flowers – to suit taste and budget

2 candles minimum

1 candlestick – to suit taste and budget

1 table cloth

1 place mat

1 each of knife, fork, spoon

1 jug (small plastic will do)

1 drinking glass

1 litre LTW (see note)

Optional:

1 glass bowl

1 bag coloured glass beads

- The first requirement is a flat, clear surface at about the height of a desk or table. Not everyone will have one of these to hand – a tall cardboard box (closed end up) will do. Cover this surface with the table cloth (a towel if nothing else). The place mat is placed on the table cloth and pressed flat to ensure a wrinkle-free surface.

- Place the cutlery on the table cloth. If you wish for a meal more dignified than artistic, the cutlery can be placed in a formal arrangement.

- Place the bunch of flowers in a container with some water. Cutting the stems at 45 degrees will help preserve many cut flowers for longer.

- Place one of the candles in the candlestick holder – if the holder is too wide, melt a few drops from the base of the candle into the holder and quickly push the candle into the wax pool: the wax will cool and hold the candle in place. Feel free to use as many candles/candlesticks as you like.

- By now, whatever you have chosen to eat (look through the rest of this book) should be prepared and ready to eat. Place the meal on a plate and the plate on the place mat.

- The final act is to add the LTW to the jug and place the jug and glass on the table cloth.

- Optional extra: for added flavour, put the lit candle in the centre of the bowl (melt the base as above to keep it stable). Gently arrange glass stones around the candle and then slowly pour in water to a tasteful depth.

- This meal is much easier to create than to describe, you might think, but to many the self-care involved in the act of inviting oneself to dinner in one's own flat will make it a difficult task. However, inviting yourself to dinner once a week and giving yourself the time you deserve can be a rewarding experience over the long term.

Note: LTW = London Tap Water. Available from most taps, this water is one of the cleanest waters available and saves on buying water in a bottle, lugging it around, drinking like a baby and then disposing of the plastic.

Broccoli and Bagna Cauda

from Elizabeth Cochrane

If you like strong flavours, then this simple dish is just perfect. I always feel I'm having something special when I make it, and yet it takes no time at all, is cheap, and involves eating an entire head of broccoli!

(serves 1)

small head of broccoli

3 tbsp olive oil

3 tinned anchovies

1–2 cloves of garlic, minced

pinch of red chilli flakes

freshly ground black pepper

- Steam the broccoli until just cooked (it should still be bright green and have a little bit of crunch).

- Meanwhile, warm the olive oil with the other ingredients over a very low heat, stirring gently to break up the anchovies.

- Dip the broccoli florets into the sauce as you eat them.

Note: If you're making it for more than one person, serve the sauce in a warmed bowl and let everyone dip into it either with the broccoli or with fresh vegetable crudités of fennel, cauliflower, peppers and courgette.

Ursula's Delicious Gazpacho

from Maki Spanoudis

This dish is a very delicious cold soup – refreshing, healthy and (surprisingly) extremely filling. My good friend Ursula made it for my mum and me, and it was superb! You do need a blender but a simple hand-held stick-type blender only costs around £10.

(serves 3)

2 cloves of garlic

250g passata

10 leaves of fresh basil

10 leaves of fresh mint

3 medium tomatoes

1 red or yellow pepper

½ a cucumber

1 small onion

2 slices dry bread

salt and pepper to taste

lemon juice (optional)

- Simply blend all the ingredients together, chill – et voilà!

Notes: Passata is puréed tomato and you can buy it in a carton or a can – it is very cheap.

You can actually serve the soup with ice cubes in it if it hasn't had enough time to chill!

Rice Salad

from Kevin Fleisch

I find many salads dull, lifeless and colourless. For this one, I use a mix of colours and textures: it's a crunchy, rainbow-looking salad. Highly nutritious, interesting, original – and it tastes different each time as the ingredients vary. Greens are tasty and really good for you. Not everywhere stocks them, so use green cabbage if you can't find them or they're out of season.

(serves 1 or more)

rice

yellow, orange, red and green peppers

greens: try collard, kale, mustard greens or turnip greens

red cabbage

red and white onions

spring onions

beetroot

long leafed lettuce

watercress

cucumber

Optional dressing:

olive oil

Manuka honey

light, low-salt soy sauce

- Rinse and boil your rice: I use long-grain wholemeal and cook with 1 measure of rice to 3 measures of water. I add a bit of margarine or butter, for the taste and to stop it sticking together, and sometimes throw in some frozen veg, plus herbs or spices. When cooked, drain the rice and chill it overnight or rinse in cold water until cold.

- Wash your vegetables and chop them into bite-sized pieces so you can eat the salad with a fork. How much of each you put in depends on what you personally like and can find or afford. Just make sure it's a mixture of reds and greens with both soft and crunchy bits: it should interest your taste buds. Add anything else salady, like celery or tomatoes or grated carrots, that's around and affordable.

- Mix everything together with the cooled rice.

- The mixture of natural tastes works really well without additions, but if you want a dressing, you can mix oil, low-salt soy sauce and honey together in 2:1:1 proportions (Manuka honey is gorgeous if you've just won the lottery!). This will keep for about two weeks in the fridge. Shake or stir vigorously before using. You will probably want to reduce the quantity of soy sauce that you use if you can't find the low-salt type.

- You can eat this on its own, or add any one of hard boiled eggs, cheese, tuna or cooked meats, again cut into bite-sized portions.

Lamb and Chickpea Goulash

from Cathy Smart

(serves 6)

olive oil

2 large onions, chopped

½ a shoulder of lamb, cubed

2 cups dried chickpeas, soaked overnight, then boiled for 1 hour

4 red and green peppers, chopped

1 aubergine, chopped

1 courgette, chopped

2 red chillies, finely chopped

4 cloves of garlic, finely chopped

1 tsp dried cinnamon

½ tsp dried nutmeg

3 tsp paprika

salt and pepper to taste

4 tins chopped tomatoes

2 tsp powdered stock

4 tsp fresh oregano or thyme

2 bay leaves

4 cups couscous

- In a large saucepan, fry the onions in a little olive oil until soft.

- Cut the meat into cubes and add to the onions. (Any lamb bones can be added to the sauce or boiled in water to make fresh stock.)

- Add the chickpeas, all the chopped vegetables and the chilli and garlic, stir in the spices and season lightly. Add the tinned tomatoes, stock and herbs and bring to boil, then simmer gently for 2 hours or transfer to a casserole dish and cook in the oven for 1½ hours on a medium heat (180 °C / gas mark 4).

- Pour boiling water on the couscous and leave until absorbed: try a ratio of 1½ measures of water to 1 measure of couscous. Fluff with a fork and then cook, covered, in the oven for 20 minutes, before serving with the goulash.

Fajitas for My Chiquito

from Ozlem Avan

This is a fun dish to cook and eat with friends. Fajitas are Mexican wraps, and you can get the ingredients from any supermarket. It's a quick recipe with no fuss and you can change it to suit your taste, just as long as you keep the secret ingredient – the mojitos! You can use Quorn pepper steaks, for example, or beef steak if you're carnivorous.

(serves 4)

1 small onion

1 each of yellow, green and sweet pointed red peppers

1 courgette

1 red chilli, finely chopped

2 cloves of garlic, finely chopped

400–600g Quorn or beef steak, sliced into strips

100g button mushrooms

fajita sauce (ready made)

To serve:

tortilla wraps

guacamole, sour cream or yoghurt, tomato salsa

- Dice all your vegetables into chunks.

- Warm a little oil in a pan, soften the onions, then add the peppers and courgettes. After a couple more minutes, add the mushrooms, chilli, garlic and steak or Quorn.

- Warm the tortillas in a very low oven. Meanwhile, drink a mojito with your guests!

- Keep stirring. Everything should be cooked but not mushy: you want a bit of crunch in your peppers. When it's done, add your fajita sauce and warm through.

- Serve the fajita mix with the warm tortillas, guacamole, sour cream and salsa, and more delicious mojitos. Each person takes a tortilla and puts a spoonful or two of the fajita mix in the middle, along with a little of each of the sauces: fold one end of the tortilla up over the filling and then one of the sides, and roll it into a wrap.

What makes a meal special?

"Love. Putting in time, beauty, creation, taste, colour, variety."

"Nice food, of course, but mostly the vibe – sometimes the food, the wine and the company gel, and a meal lasts for five hours. Those are the best."

"The company, always: if you're cooking, you're feeding those you love and making them feel special. If you're being cooked for, it's feeling that someone else has made an effort for you."

"The love of food and good ingredients."

"It is real enjoyment seeing people happily gobbling up the food you've carefully cooked for them."

Quinoa Salad

With its green leaves and broccoli florets, plus the red onion and pomegranate seeds, this is a beautifully colourful salad. It will serve 6 quite greedy people as a main course or more as a side dish.

(serves 6–10)

2 litres water

400 g quinoa

vegetable stock cube

200 g steamed broccoli florets

large handful of spinach leaves, chopped

1 cucumber, peeled and diced

1 small red onion, finely sliced

seeds of half a pomegranate

handful of brazil nuts,
roughly chopped

4 tbsp olive oil

1 tbsp honey

3 tbsp balsamic vinegar

salt and pepper

- Place the quinoa in a pan with the water and stock cube and leave to simmer for 25–30 minutes, until the grains have doubled in size and look like transparent little pearls; leave to rest for 5 minutes.

- Rinse the quinoa in a sieve under cold water and drain well. Place in a bowl and combine with the vegetables, pomegranate seeds and nuts.

- Whisk together the olive oil, honey and balsamic vinegar in a separate bowl and season lightly. Mix this dressing in with the quinoa.

Note: Quinoa is a very nutritious grain-like food which you can use like rice. Along with fibre, iron and various minerals, it's high in protein, and actually provides a complete protein, making it great for vegetarians.

Slow-Cooked Pork Tongue

from David Burnett, mentor to CoolTan Arts

They virtually give tongues away at a decent butcher, and this recipe – which fits brilliantly into the whole trend for slow food – actually only takes about 3 minutes of work if you have the stock ready in your freezer: you can put the dish in the oven at breakfast time and it will be absolutely delicious by dinner time.

(serves 4)

4 pigs' tongues

chicken stock

1 tsp Chinese five-spice powder

½ a handful of dried porcini mushrooms

- Take the pigs' tongues, and cover with good, well reduced chicken stock made from the carcass of a roast chicken, to which you have added the Chinese five-spice powder and the porcini mushrooms.

- Cook slowly, either in a slow cooker or for several hours in a well sealed casserole dish in a very low oven (120 °C / gas mark ½).

- Eat with greens and crusty bread.

Note: Chinese five-spice powder is a mixture of star anise, cloves, cinnamon, Sichuan pepper and fennel seeds (sometimes ginger is included in place of fennel). The idea is that it includes all five tastes: sweet, sour, bitter, pungent, and salty.

FEEDING THE VILLAGE

At a party or a picnic, food draws people together.
Whether with family, friends, or people you've never
met, it's a way to create community.

Broccoli and Chicken Lasagne

This is an easy version of lasagne, as you don't have to make a béchamel sauce. The recipe is easily extended or adapted: experiment with different vegetables and herbs. To make it vegetarian, you can replace the meat with mushrooms, tofu or similar.

(serves 4)

500 g broccoli, washed and chopped

500 g chicken/turkey breasts

4 tbsp rapeseed oil

50 g butter

1 red onion, finely chopped

2 cloves of garlic, crushed

3 cups passata (sieved creamed tomatoes)

2 sprigs each of thyme and oregano

12 sheets of pre-cooked lasagne

½ cup fromage frais

100 g grated parmesan cheese

250 g mozzarella cheese, thinly sliced

- Pre-heat the oven to 180 °C / gas mark 4 and butter a large shallow ovenproof dish.

- Steam the broccoli until nearly tender, then strain and set aside.

- Cut the chicken or turkey into thin strips and season lightly with black pepper and salt. Heat the oil and butter in a frying pan and gently brown the meat, then transfer it onto a plate.

- Add the onion and garlic to the pan and fry for 3–4 minutes until the onion has softened and is light golden brown. Stir in the passata, thyme, oregano and seasoning, and cook for about 5 minutes over a moderate heat, stirring regularly, until the sauce is slightly thickened.

- Spoon half the tomato sauce into the prepared dish and add a layer of 4 lasagne sheets, then half the chicken and broccoli. Dot with half the fromage frais and then sprinkle with half the parmesan. Place another layer of 4 lasagne sheets on top and spoon over the remaining tomato sauce, chicken or turkey, broccoli and fromage frais.

- Add a last layer of lasagne, arrange the slices of mozzarella cheese on top and sprinkle with the remaining parmesan.

- Bake for 40 minutes until the top is golden. Serve with a watercress salad.

Yemeni White Fish with Red Pepper and Spices

from Shada Hussein

In Yemen, food is one of the ways a family shows unity. Lunch is the main meal of the day. All of the family members gather to eat, but no one starts until the head of the family – who could be the father or the mother or the grandfather – starts. People treat each other kindly and feed one another: usually they are sitting on the floor with the food in the middle, and everybody eats from the main dish.

(serves 6)

8 to 12 cloves garlic, peeled but whole

2 red peppers, cut into in chunks

1 tsp cumin (or to taste)

½ tsp turmeric (or to taste)

salt and freshly ground pepper to taste

1–2 tbsp vegetable oil

100 ml water

1.5 kg white fish: use whiting, sea bass or trout fillets

paprika to taste

- Put the garlic, red pepper, cumin, turmeric, salt, pepper, oil and water in a saucepan and simmer very slowly, covered, for about 1½ hours. Be careful not to let the sauce burn, adding water if necessary.

- Pour some of the sauce into a baking pan and place the fish on top. Spoon the rest of the sauce around the fish.

- Cover and place in a low oven or on top of the stove for 15–20 minutes or until the fish flakes easily.

- Serve on a large plate with a pile of rice in the centre and the fish and sauce all around it, sprinkled with paprika.

How do you cope if you have to cook for a lot of people?

"I love it. I have to start early though, so that the experience is an enjoyable one!"

"Messily. I can only really manage it if I pretend I'm on a TV cooking show and do loads of prep so all the ingredients are in neat little bowls. Otherwise I panic."

"Prepare your favourite pots and special equipment, and do some of the boring tasks that take a long time (e.g. veg preparation, rice), the night before. Believe me, it saves time – and you can attend to your loved guests for longer!"

"Do simple, big things with lots of veg so people can help themselves and tuck in. Plus lots of pudding, and lots of wine."

"I love it. It's a big wonderful stress, and a great opportunity to experiment with complicated new recipes."

"I am usually relaxed. Since my college days I've been asked by friends to cook Indian meals for them. I can cope with cooking for up to about 30 people, so long as it's at their place and not at my place. I rarely invite people to my place."

Mrs B's Swedish Meatballs

from Ulrika Bygge

Hearty and warming, meatballs are pretty much Sweden's national dish, eaten all year round. This particular recipe is my mother's version and it reminds me of when I was a kid, excitedly pressing my face against the window, longing to get back out in the snow. I love getting messy rolling the mixture into balls and usually get friends involved in the rolling too! Make sure you serve them with plenty of lingonberry jam – the mixture of savoury meat and bitter-sweet, zingy jam is delicious.

This takes just 15 minutes to prepare and 30 minutes to cook. It should make about 50–60 meatballs, which would serve 6–8 people as a main dish, or more alongside other foods. I usually make a large batch as it doesn't matter if you don't eat them all – they're great to put in the freezer and defrost as and when you get that meatball craving!

(serves 6–8)

1 kg minced beef

2 onions, finely chopped

1 egg

½ cup breadcrumbs

75 ml milk

1 tsp salt

½ tsp black pepper

a few knobs of butter for frying

- Mix all the ingredients together in a bowl and work them thoroughly with your hands.

- Using a pair of spoons dipped in water (so the mixture doesn't stick to them), shape the mass into balls and lay these aside on a chopping board. Alternatively get right in there and roll the balls between the palms of your hands!

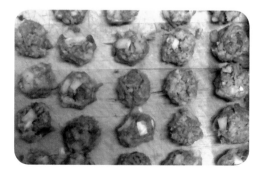 

- Fry the balls quite slowly in the butter until they are golden brown. You will have to fry them in batches as they won't all fit in the frying pan at the same time. Once each batch is ready, put them in a heatproof dish and keep them warm in the oven on a very low heat.

- Serve with mashed potatoes, gravy and lingonberry jam.

Note: You can get lingonberry jam along with lots of other Swedish goodies at the Totally Swedish shop in Marylebone – or at Ikea!

Cooking for Friends is my Meditation

Sasha McSean

Cooking has been important to me since I was a child. I was brought up with no siblings by my father, a single parent. He always cooked for me and started teaching me to cook at a young age. I lived in a multicultural town and when Dad was working I spent a lot of time at friends' houses. I loved having my friends' Indian and Caribbean mums feeding me up. I often got in their way asking questions in the kitchen. As an only child it helped me feel part of a family. Cooking is a good way to share love and nourish the soul.

For my 10th birthday I announced I wanted to cook for the family. My family was very fragmented. I invited all those I loved and although they did not like each other they all came together for one day for the love of a 10-year-old and her feast. I made a five-course meal, with a properly laid table and music, and I still remember what I cooked: beef stroganoff and chocolate roulade – all from scratch, with no help!

By the age of 15 I was living alone. I realised I could not afford to eat well unless I bought fresh in bulk and cooked in bulk. At 36, I still do this, and I now have 4 freezers that are filled with home-cooked food. I share this with friends, who often travel far to eat my meals, and there are many dishes of my own creation that have become regular favourites.

I am suffering from fibromyalgia, among other conditions, and have struggled in the past with depression. Cooking not only allows me to socialise, encouraging friends to visit when I'm not mobile enough to join in their activities, but also allows me to give back a big thank you to those that help me with the chores I'm unable to do myself. It makes me feel more independent and useful as my friends cannot cook very well and often don't eat good quality food. I'm giving them something they need and love in return for their help instead of just being a dependant 'disabled' friend. I have taught many a kitchen virgin upon request, and they even take packed versions of dishes for their lunches and freezers.

Most importantly, when I'm suffering from extreme pain and don't want to get out of bed or talk to anyone, cooking is the only solace I can find. On days when it's difficult to socialise or think clearly, the creativity and freedom of cooking provide an easier way to engage. I will cook even when I don't want to eat. I get lost in the creativity, the sounds and smells; I feel the same satisfaction an artist must feel when their painting is complete, the same absorption during the task. Cooking is my meditation.

Vegetable Gratin

from Sasha McSean

You will need a very large saucepan and at least 2 large, deep, square casserole/lasagne type glass oven dishes. I cook by sight, taste and smell, not measurements, so these amounts are a rough guide – play with the recipe to find the balance you like. There are only 2 rules: the onions and the courgettes must be of equal amounts, and the topping must adequately cover the filling with no gaps. Please try to use organic where possible: it really does make a difference to the taste. The dish freezes well too: if freezing, take it out of the oven when it's still turning golden, not after it has turned.

(serves 16)

For the filling:

16–20 courgettes, depending on size, grated

8–10 large or 12 medium onions, very thinly sliced

2 yellow peppers, thinly sliced

6–8 tbsp sesame oil

1 tbsp caraway seeds

2 tbsp dried thyme (not crucial if you can't get it)

4–6 fresh or frozen bay leaves, not dried

splash of tarragon white wine vinegar

75–100 ml ginger juice

1½–2 tins chopped tomatoes

For the topping:

1 tsp Maldon sea salt

12 large eggs (use more if medium sized)

splash of milk

250–300 g strong cheddar cheese, grated (or less if you like)

½ cup sesame seeds

½ cup shelled hemp seeds

To serve:

straight-to-wok medium noodles   (medium work better than large or ribbon noodles)

soy sauce to taste

- Prepare your vegetables and pre-heat the oven to 200 °C / gas mark 6.

- Heat the sesame oil in the pan. When it's warm, add the onions with the caraway seeds, thyme and bay leaves. Don't brown the onions, just soften them. When they look a bit glassy, add the peppers and fry a few minutes more until they also soften.

- Stir in the grated courgettes, cook for another couple of minutes, then stir in the ginger juice and splash a little tarragon vinegar evenly over.

- Allow the mixture to cook for a further minute or two without stirring. It should 'relax' down by maybe a centimetre and start to look 'damp' from the juices released. The individual vegetables should be barely distinguishable now. Stir in the tomatoes, turn up the heat for a minute or two, then turn it off.

- Put the courgette mixture into the oven dish and flatten it down a bit so that the egg will sit on top rather than mixing in. There will be some 'gravy', which is fine. You can sprinkle a thin layer of cheese over the veggies if you like, but not too much.

- Whisk the eggs lightly, adding just a splash of milk. Pour the egg mixture over the vegetables gently and evenly, then sprinkle the cheese over. There should be enough depth to the dish to let the egg topping rise a little.

- Cover the dish with foil or a lid and put it in the oven, on the middle or top shelf.

- Check the dish after 7–10 minutes. Once the top looks sealed enough to take their weight, sprinkle the seeds generously over it. Discard the foil and continue to cook till you can smell the food. You're just waiting for the egg and cheese to turn into an omelette topping. A glass dish allows you to watch the process under the seeds.

- A few minutes before you think it's ready, get a non-stick wok quite hot and toss the noodles in with your fingers from a height (you don't need any oil). Stir-fry these a few minutes, adding a splash of soy sauce to taste.

- Serve in a bowl with a slice of gratin on top of the noodles. Eat with chopsticks.

Notes: You can use crumbled feta in place of cheddar for a fluffier, lighter topping.

As someone who cooks regularly in large quantities I always have large balls of frozen chopped garlic and ginger. When making these balls, I pour the juice from the ginger into small ramekins and freeze it separately. You can purée ginger root as an alternative.

Hemp seeds are rich in omega oils, and found in all good health-food shops. Note that our picture shows unshelled hemp seeds, which are not the best option!

Dips for a Picnic

from Kathrin Kirrmann

Obatzda and Kartoffelkas are cheese specialities from Bavaria, South Germany. We serve them with dark rye bread, fresh pretzels (Brezn) or fresh vegetables such as red radish, carrots or whatever you fancy. These snacks are easy and quick to make, and they are perfect for parties or, even better, to take out in the beer garden or to picnics to share with friends. That's what I used to do: make some Obatzda, take some veg and then join some friends in the beer garden for a nice chat in the sun or under beautiful trees, with a cool Bavarian beer, Brezn, Obatzda, Kartoffelkas and vegetables. Forget any problems and enjoy the moment!

Obatzda

(serves 4)

1 small onion

450 g mature Brie or Camembert

2 tbsp soft butter

1 tbsp beer

3 tbsp cream cheese

1 tsp paprika

1 tsp ground cumin

salt and white pepper

½ a bunch of chives, finely chopped

- Peel the onion and cut it in half. Chop one half finely. Slice the rest into fine half-rings.

- With a fork, soften the Brie or Camembert in a small bowl. Add the butter, beer and cream cheese and mix well.

- Add the finely chopped onion and season the mix with paprika, cumin, salt and pepper. Mix well, cover and refrigerate for an hour.

- Serve the Obatzda with the chives and onion slices scattered over the top, along with freshly baked bread or pretzels, and fresh, crunchy crudités.

Kartoffelkas

(serves 4)

450 g floury potatoes

1 medium onion, finely diced

½ cup cream

½ cup sour cream or crème fraîche

salt

freshly ground pepper

freshly ground nutmeg

- Boil the potatoes in salted water for 20–25 minutes until soft. Drain and let cool.

- Peel the potatoes and press them through a potato ricer if you have one, or a colander if you don't, into a bowl. (It's also ok just to mash them until they are very smooth.)

- Add the cream and the sour cream to the potatoes and mix until smooth.

- Add the onion to the potato spread and season to taste with salt, pepper and nutmeg. Mix well, then refrigerate for an hour.

- Spread the Kartoffelkas on rye bread, garnished with chopped chives or parsley, onion rings and radishes.

Baba Ghanoush

Baba ghanoush is a smoky aubergine dip, delicious with wholewheat bread, pita or crackers, or spread in sandwiches with salad.

There are many ways to cook the aubergines for this dish. You can roast them whole: pierce the skins, wrap them in foil and roast in a very hot oven for 35–40 minutes. Alternatively, charring the skins will give them a good smoky flavour: cut the aubergines in half and grill them, cut side down, until the skin is blackened and the flesh soft. You can even hold the aubergine over the flame on a gas hob and char the surface section by section.

(serves 12)

2 largish aubergines

10 tbsp tahini

3–4 cloves of garlic, crushed

juice of 1 large lemon

pinch of cumin powder

pinch of salt

coriander leaves

olive oil

- Cook the aubergines and let them cool, then scoop out the softened flesh, squeeze it to remove any excess water, roughly chop it and purée with the tahini. You can discard the skins.

- Mix in the crushed garlic, lemon juice, cumin powder and salt: the exact quantities depend on your taste.

- Add a little water if the mixture feels too stiff: it should be smooth and delicious.

- Leave to sit for a while so that the flavours can mellow and blend.

- To serve, drizzle with olive oil and add fresh coriander leaves (or mint or parsley, if you prefer) to taste.

Hot Fennel and Tomato Soup

from Rosemary Shrager, patron of CoolTan Arts

A perfect recipe for taking on a long walk – like the CoolTan Arts Largactyl Shuffle!

(serves 4)

2 tbsp olive oil

2 bulbs fennel

450 g fresh ripe tomatoes

2 cloves of garlic

275 ml V8 juice or tomato juice

grated rind of ½ a lemon

salt and pepper

½ tsp white sugar

275 ml chicken stock

a 400 g tin of butterbeans, drained and rinsed

- Wash and chop the fennel, reserving the fronds.

- Heat the oil in a thick pan, add the fennel and cook over a gentle heat for 10 minutes until soft but not browned, stirring occasionally.

- Meanwhile, peel the tomatoes, plunging them first for 1 minute in boiling water (this helps to loosen the skins). Roughly chop them.

- Crush the garlic into the fennel, stir round and cook for 1 minute, then add the tomatoes, V8 juice, lemon rind, salt, pepper, sugar and chicken stock. Bring to the boil and simmer for 5 minutes. Take off the heat and liquidize or process the soup.

- Return the soup to a clean pan and stir the butterbeans through. Chop the reserved fennel fronds and add also.

- Bring to boiling point, test for seasoning and add a little more stock if it is too thick for your taste (this will depend a lot on how watery your tomatoes are).

- When it's fully heated through, put the soup into a thermos flask which has been previously heated with boiling water.

Cooking for CoolTan Arts

Asia Wieloch

CoolTan Arts is a multicultural community. Many of us come from different countries, have different cultural backgrounds and ethnicities. Sharing food is an important aspect of community life, and so at CoolTan Arts we like to celebrate various events by sharing meals together. Often we organise a get-together where everyone brings something from their country, or food that has particular significance for them or that they especially like to eat.

More recently we have introduced the idea of events where we actually prepare the food at CoolTan Arts for all our participants, volunteers, staff and friends. It is always a big party as there are many of us here at CoolTan. Our dream is to have a proper kitchen and a café where we can serve food for everyone. We do not have the best kitchen facilities in the world, but this doesn't stop us from cooking together.

Vegetarian 'Chopped Liver' Pâté

from Asia Wieloch

This vegetarian pâté or paste can be eaten with crackers, toast or chopped raw vegetables. There are lots of ways of making it, but they all involve hard-boiled eggs and sautéed onion along with some kind of vegetable such as beans, mushrooms or – as here – aubergine.

(serves 12–14)

2 medium aubergines

½ cup flour (optional)

sunflower oil

1 medium onion, chopped

2 cloves of garlic, chopped

3 hard-boiled eggs

pinch of salt

black pepper

- Peel the aubergines and cut into ½-inch slices. Sprinkle these with salt, leave for 20 minutes to let them release some juice, then rinse, and dry with kitchen paper.

- Sprinkle the aubergine slices with flour and fry until dark brown on both sides (drain on kitchen paper afterwards). Alternatively, you can grill them. Set them aside to cool.

- Sauté the chopped onions and garlic over a medium heat until softened (but not too brown).

- Place the aubergine, onions and garlic in a food processor. Add the hard-boiled eggs and season with salt and pepper. Process until the spread is smooth.

Marinated Carrots à la CoolTan

from Kathrin Kirrmann

Easy, cheap, popular... and orange! Perfect for parties or BBQs.

(serves 8–10)

1 kg carrots

3 cloves of garlic, finely chopped or crushed in a garlic press

3 tbsp olive oil

1–2 tbsp vegetable oil

3 tbsp balsamic vinegar

1 tbsp white wine or red wine vinegar

1 tsp dried oregano

salt

chilli powder or cayenne pepper to taste

pinch of sugar

- Peel the carrots, quarter them length-wise, then slice those sticks into 3 cm-long pieces.

- Boil a pan of water, add a pinch of salt, then put the carrots into it and cook for 5–6 minutes.

- Strain the carrots and rinse them with cold water to cool.

- Put the carrots in a big bowl, add all the other ingredients and mix.

- Put this in the fridge for at least 6 hours, ideally overnight. Don't taste the carrots until they've had a chance to marinate: they need time to absorb the flavours to taste good.

Curried Lentil Soup

from Cheryl, a CoolTan Arts volunteer

This recipe originates from India. It gives a warm and comfortable feeling because of the spices used. The ingredients used are easy to obtain and provide fibre and B vitamins; lentils are also a useful source of iron, which we all need plenty of. Garlic is said by some people to be an aphrodisiac!

(serves 4)

oil for frying

2 carrots, peeled and chopped

3 celery sticks, sliced

1 onion, chopped

1 tbsp curry powder

¼ tsp ground coriander

¼ tsp ground cumin

1 clove of garlic, crushed

1 litre vegetable stock

1 tbsp tomato purée

125 g lentils, washed

3 large potatoes, peeled and grated

salt and black pepper

- Sauté the carrots, celery and onion until soft.

- Add the curry powder, coriander, cumin and garlic and fry for a further 2 minutes.

- Add the stock, tomato purée, lentils and potato and simmer for 30–40 minutes.

- Season with salt and pepper and serve with naan bread or chapattis.

Pumpkin Soup

from Emine Mustafa

The great thing about soup is that quantities of each ingredient are seldom crucial – you can be pretty flexible.

(serves 6)

1 pumpkin, or piece of pumpkin, of about 2 kg

1 potato

1 carrot

1 stick of celery

1 onion

1 clove of garlic

juice of ½ a lemon

salt and pepper

- Clean the pumpkin of seeds, remove the skin with a sharp knife, and roughly chop the flesh.

- Peel the other vegetables and chop them into small pieces. Crush or finely chop the garlic.

- Put all the vegetables in a pan with water covering them by about an inch, and bring to the boil.

- Add the lemon juice and season with salt and pepper, then turn down the heat and simmer till the vegetables are cooked. This will probably take 25–30 minutes.

- You can blend or mash it if you want a smooth soup, but it's not necessary, as the vegetables should be soft anyway and it tastes just as good when it's a bit chunky.

Note: Try varying this recipe by using the juice of half an orange instead of the lemon juice, or adding a ½-inch piece of ginger root, finely chopped.

SWEET TREATS

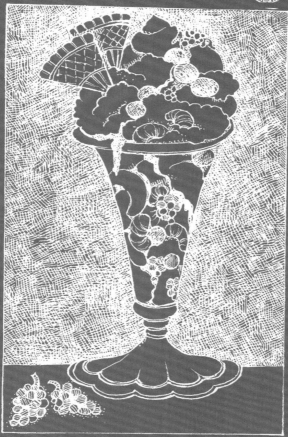

Biscuits for a visitor, birthday cakes, a fruity pudding to round off a meal: a little of what you fancy does you good!

Jam Tomorrow

a poem by Peter Cox

Jam tomorrow but none today. Confiture demain, mais pas aujourd'hui.

Today we have Marmite, houmous, tzatziki, garlic butter, peanut butter, sandwich spread, satay sauce, chutney, cheese from a tube, honey and lemon curd. But for jam, cranberry sauce and marmalade, come tomorrow. Come to our Jamfest with so many kinds of jam that some will never wish to see jam again while others will become jamoholics, jam round their mouths, perhaps even having been MASSAGED with jam, courtesy of Jamotherapy.

Come to our jamming session. Jamming is the informal playing of musical instruments by groups while eating things with jam in them. So there will be jam butties, jam tarts, jam rolls and jam sponge cake. Join Jammy Jimmy, who jams in his jimjams. Jam to songs like Mamma Mia, Thank You For The Jam, Strawberry Jam For Ever, Jam Balaya, The Jambusters and I'm Going To Wash That Jam Right Out Of My Hair. Buy seedless jam from Wobblies of Wimbledon. Learn about the Artful Dodger, a jam addict who was the inspiration for the word jammy and the famous biscuit named the Jammie Dodger. And at Poetry Corner, Marma-lady reads her poetry. Here is a sample of the great stuff that got her voted Poet Laureate:

The rain in Spain stays up the hill
and I am going to Seville.
Wham bim bam, I thank you, Ma'am
for giving me a pot of jam.

Or try to unjam a door jammed by the stickiest of jams. Will the door come unstuck, or will YOU?

Our Jamfest ends with all joining sticky hands for a raucous rendition of
Auld Lang Jam.

Queen of Hearts Jam Tarts

from Sara Burgess

These are very easy and quick to make, and produce a plentiful amount of sweet treats. They remind me of the 'Queen of Hearts' tale from Alice in Wonderland. You can make your own pastry, though it makes a bit more mess in the kitchen. The recipe makes as many as you want.

ready-made shortcrust pastry

strawberry jam

- Roll out the pastry and cut out circles using a pastry cutter or similar round object.

- Grease a 12-cup baking pan. Put the pastry circles into the dips to make cup shapes.

- Put a teaspoon of jam into each pastry case.

- With a sharp knife, cut out shapes from the remaining pastry – for example hearts or stars – and place these on top of the tarts.

- Bake for 20 minutes at 190 °C / gas mark 5, until just golden.

- Allow them to cool (very important as the jam will be extremely hot!) then serve.

Note: If any are left over then they can be frozen.

Rhubarb and Raspberry Crumble

from Pablo Antoli

For the crumble topping:

250 g plain flour, sifted

125 g butter, at room temperature, cut into small pieces

75 g light brown soft sugar

75 g demerara sugar

For the filling:

500 g trimmed rhubarb, cut into chunks

150 g raspberries, fresh or frozen

2 tsp cornflour

2 tsp sugar

- Pre-heat the oven to 180 °C / gas mark 4.

- First, make the topping. Place the flour in a large mixing bowl, then add the butter and rub it into the flour lightly, using your fingertips.

- When it all looks crumbly and the fat has been dispersed fairly evenly, add the sugar and combine that well with the rest.

- To make the filling, mix rhubarb, raspberries, sugar and cornflour. Place this mix in a baking dish.

- Spoon the crumble over and bake for 30–40 minutes.

- Serve with custard, chilled pouring cream or vanilla ice cream.

How do you feel about puddings?

"There's more magic to baking than to regular cooking."

"How do I feel about puddings? That there should be lots of them, and always dark chocolate to go with coffee or tea after supper."

"I'm reluctant to make too many sweet things for fear of eating them."

"I love ice cream!"

Ginger Sponge

from Marjorie McLean

This recipe contains no eggs or dairy.

100 g margarine
75 g (3 level tbsp) golden syrup
140 ml boiling water
225 g self-raising flour
1 tsp bicarbonate of soda
2 tsp ground ginger
1 tsp mixed spice
100 g caster sugar
or soft dark brown sugar

- Pre-heat the oven to 160°C / gas mark 3.

- Line a 20 cm round or 18 cm square tin (should be 4 cm deep) with baking paper and grease it.

- Place the margarine and golden syrup in a small basin. Pour over the boiling water and leave until the margarine has melted, stirring if necessary.

- Sift the flour, bicarbonate of soda, ginger and mixed spice into a bowl. Stir in the sugar.

- Make a well in the centre, pour in the syrup mixture and, with a wooden spoon, beat until smooth. Pour into the prepared tin and bake above the centre of the oven for about 35 minutes or until firm and springy. Cool in the tin.

- Keeps well in an air-tight tin for up to 2 weeks. You can also freeze it for up to 3 months, wrapped in cling film or a plastic bag.

Shortbread

from Cheryl, a CoolTan Arts volunteer

It must have been just before my teens when I caught the baking bug. Me and my sister were forever looking at our mother's huge collection of recipe cards and cutting out and keeping the recipes from the Women's Weeklies she bought. I used to watch Farmhouse Kitchen and be fascinated by silly little things like eggs being whisked. We assisted our mother in making our traditional Black Cake every Christmas, but the day my mother let me loose in her kitchen to make fairy cakes on my own was a complete disaster. I just couldn't do no right! In the end, the kitchen was a tip. I was not easily deterred by that experience though and eventually made more fairy cakes, progressing on to scones, rock cakes, biscuits, family and celebratory cakes, sponges and also simple confectionary.

100g butter

50g caster sugar

175g plain flour, sifted

caster sugar for dredging

- Cream the butter and sugar until light and fluffy.

- Add the flour and stir until the mixture binds together.

- Turn onto a lightly floured board and knead until smooth.

- Roll out into a 20 cm circle and place it onto a greased baking sheet. Pinch the edges of the circle with your fingers, prick all over with a fork and mark into 8 portions.

- Dust lightly with caster sugar and bake in a pre-heated oven at 160°C / gas mark 3 for 40–45 minutes until pale golden.

- Leave on the sheet for 5 minutes before transferring to a wire rack to cool completely. Serve with tea or coffee.

Cheesecake

from Michelle's grandad

675 g cream cheese

4 eggs

6 tbsp caster sugar

1 carton sour cream

1 tbsp cornflour

juice and rind of 1 lemon

about half a pack of digestive biscuits

- Grease a 20 cm cake tin.

- Put the digestive biscuits in a plastic bag and crush them to crumbs with a rolling pin or something similar. Then turn the crumbs out into the bottom of the cake tin and press them down to make the cheesecake base.

- Whisk up all the other ingredients thoroughly in a bowl and pour into the cake tin. Bake the cake for 45 minutes at 180 °C / gas mark 4 and then turn the gas off and leave the cake in the oven overnight. (You might want to put a baking tray under the cake tin while it's baking to stop anything from spilling out onto the oven.)

Chai Brownies

from Amos Philips

2 tbsp unsweetened cocoa powder

30 g unsweetened desiccated coconut

125 g plain flour

200 g caster sugar

4 tbsp unsweetened cocoa powder

½ tsp baking powder

½ tsp salt

125 ml very strongly brewed chai tea

125 ml rapeseed oil

½ tsp vanilla extract

- Pre-heat the oven to 180 °C / gas mark 4.

- Spray a 20 cm square baking tin with cooking spray (or grease lightly with oil or butter) and dust lightly with the 2 tablespoons of cocoa powder.

- Place the coconut in a food processor, pulse until finely chopped, and set aside.

- Whisk together the flour, sugar, 4 tablespoons of cocoa powder, baking powder and salt.

- Stir in the brewed chai, rapeseed oil and vanilla extract, just until all the ingredients are moistened.

- Fold in the coconut. Spread the batter in the prepared pan.

- Bake in the pre-heated oven until the top is no longer shiny – about 20 minutes.

- Allow to cool for 1 hour before cutting.

Note: Make sure you use vegan sugar if you want the finished product to be 100 % vegan.

Lemony Poppy Seed Cake

from Peter Detre's recipe collection

120 g butter

3 large eggs

200 g caster sugar

130 g self-raising flour

170 g plain yoghurt

1 tsp vanilla essence

4 tbsp poppy seeds

zest of 2 lemons

For the syrup:

juice of 2 lemons

4 tbsp icing sugar

- Pre-heat the oven to 180 °C / gas mark 4. Grease a 24 cm cake tin or ovenproof dish and line with greaseproof paper or a cake tin liner.

- Melt the butter.

- Beat eggs and sugar together till light and fluffy. Mix in the melted butter.

- Add the flour and mix well, then add the yoghurt, vanilla, poppy seeds and lemon zest. Mix well.

- Pour into the prepared tin and bake for 35 minutes or so, until a toothpick inserted into the centre comes out clean.

- While the cake is baking, make the syrup: heat the lemon juice and icing sugar in a small saucepan until the sugar is dissolved.

- Take the cake out of the oven, spike all over with a skewer. Pour the syrup over it (it will run down into the skewer holes) and leave the cake in the tin to cool.

Note: The cake may sink in the middle when cool. It doesn't affect the taste! Disguise by dusting with icing sugar before serving.

Peter Detre was a mentor to CoolTan Arts, and famous for his love of cooking.

CUP OF JOY

Cool, fizzy drinks refresh us; a mug of something warm and sweet can soothe you to sleep. A break from work, a meal in itself, a celebration: there's a drink here for every occasion.

Summer Drinks

from Claudia Young

Summer evenings are the perfect time to relax with a glass of something delicious. Creating non-alcoholic cocktails can be really fun: the best way is to mix and match until you have the perfect combination of tastes. Here are some useful tips to get started.

Fruit-based drinks, often with a bit of fizz thrown in, are really refreshing. If you're making grown-up soft drinks for lots of people, big jugs are easier – and quick to top up. Start with ice and lots of it. Pour over a good fruit juice or cordial, and top up with about 5 times as much fizzy or still water. It looks lovely, and tastes delicious, if you add some fresh fruit pieces and/or herbs as well.

Some interesting combinations:

- Cloudy apple juice, topped up with sparkling water, garnished with lots of fresh mint.

- Any fruit cordial with soda water and redcurrants and/or blueberries on top.

- Orange juice and lemonade looks like something special with slices of orange and maybe fresh raspberries added to it.

- Cranberry and pineapple juice with lime pieces is fresh and tropical!

- Classic elderflower cordial is perfect with either sparkling or still water – and a couple of halved strawberries makes it even more summery.

Ginger ale and iced tea are both good bases for cocktails. Try:

- Ginger ale with slices of fresh apple and wedges of lime.

- Equal parts ginger ale, orange juice and cranberry juice, with a squeeze of lemon juice.

- The American favourite, the 'half-and-half': it's half lemonade and half iced tea. With a sprig of mint or few fresh raspberries thrown in, it's even better.

- Iced tea with a glug each of pineapple juice, orange juice and lemonade.

Of course, there are some classic flavour combinations, like elderflower and apple, ginger and lime, mango and orange – but you can also make more exotic mixes: how about lychee juice with crushed strawberries, soda water and mint leaves? When pomegranates are cheap, you can pile their beautiful red seeds into real lemonade – again, with some mint sprigs. Sometimes supermarkets sell borage amongst their fresh herbs: it's surprisingly delicious in summer drinks, especially with strawberries. And cucumber makes even plain still water taste delicate and delicious. There are so many things to try: surprise yourself, and enjoy summer!

Green Juice

If you have access to a juicer or blender, you can make an endless array of tasty, healthy, creative drinks – some of which can be as filling as a small meal. Some people swear by them as a way to start the day, but you could also create colourful cocktails for serving to friends.

You can pretty well mix together anything that's cheap and in season, including vegetables like cauliflower, broccoli, cabbage and lettuce. Some of these taste rather bitter by themselves, but are delicious when mixed with sweeter things such as apples, carrots or beetroot (this also increases the range of vitamins you're consuming). If you find them and can afford them, you can include nutrient-rich ingredients such as wheat grass, barley grass and alfalfa. Experiment with adding ginger, basil, mint and other tasty flavourings – there's no end to the juices you can create!

Here are some combinations to get you started:

- 4 cups of kale, half a cucumber, three sticks of celery, 2–4 apples: it's a power juice, this one, as kale is very healthy!

- 4 bananas, 1 mango, 2 dates: this one's thick and sweet, like a smoothie – and since it makes quite a lot, you can share it. Thin it out with yoghurt or juice if you like.

- 2 or 3 spinach leaves, 2 celery sticks, a handful of parsley, 3 apples, ½ a cucumber, a slice of ginger: it's sweet and lively.

- How about a fresh salad-drink? Try a combination of spinach, parsley, celery, cucumber, lettuce (romaine is good), alfalfa sprouts and mint.

- In the winter, take a root boost: mix beetroot, swede, turnip and radishes with a bit of cucumber for freshness.

You don't need to peel all your green fruits and vegetables – just rinse things like apples and cucumbers as necessary. And don't worry too much about quantities of the various ingredients: there's no correct way to combine them, so long as you enjoy the result. Do drink your juice soon after making it though, as the vitamin content starts to degrade with time – or you can freeze any extra in tupperware.

Uplifting Mood

Sandhya Kaffo

There is a level of excitement that comes with creating a recipe from scratch. This affects foodies particularly, but it can become infectious to others too if you're really passionate about food.

I feel like an artist with an empty canvas, accompanied by painting pots full of the rainbow colours of fruits and vegetables, along with the myriad of spices and herbs that lend their power to shift the flavour of the emerging dish. This process of creating a dish uplifts my mood in the same way an artist would experience on completing a rare painting to his satisfaction – and the dish need not be complex, by the way. Perhaps I could liken my 'recipe paintings' to a Pollock: abstract, inventive, exploratory and freeing. They're visually pleasing and fabulously delicious, appealing to all the senses. The delight on people's faces after a taste or two also leaves my heart as warm and cosy as a hot cup of cardamom seed milk. Yum!

Cardamom Seed Milk

from Sandhya Kaffo

(serves 2)

1 cup sunflower seeds

2 cups boiled water

2 whole green cardamom pods

1 tsp honey or sweetener of choice

- Blend in a high-speed blender.

- Sieve through a fine mesh sieve or cheesecloth.

- Pour milky liquid into a glass.

- Drink and be very merry indeed.

Note: Rather than honey, I use a spicy sweet Indian blend called Chywanprakash in my recipe. It's not vegan (it contains ghee) but it is very healthy – full of vitamin C!

Warm Cardamom Milk

You can also flavour cow's milk with the warm sweet taste of cardamom to make a delicious night-time drink.

(serves 2)

500 ml milk

10 cardamom pods

1–2 tsp sugar

- Heat the milk until just simmering, then add the sugar and cardamom pods (slightly crushed, so the seeds can come out), take off the heat and let steep for 20 minutes.

- Heat through again, strain and serve.

Tea or coffee?

"Tea can be very nice, usually if someone else makes it for me. Coffee is my passion and addiction."

"I drink Yogi herbal teas comfortably. I make tea from raw ginger and honey, sometimes with lemon too. Maybe once a month I drink coffee, but I always feel guilty while doing this – for health reasons."

"Tea and coffee? I drink them too much – but I love them both. Tea is like a hug, and coffee is like a kick in the pants."

"Coffee to wake up. Tea in the afternoon. Peppermint tea before bed."

Moroccan Mint Tea

from Abdellah Smita

We can't speak about Morocco without mentioning green tea with mint, because it's so popular. It's often served after couscous, with honey pastries.

(serves 8)

3 heaped tbsp Oolong tea

2 heaped tbsp dried mint leaves (or a big handful of fresh mint)

½ cup sugar

- Pour boiling water into a glass or china teapot, rinse it out and throw the water away (this heats the pot).

- Put the loose tea (do not use teabags) into the pot with the mint and the sugar, and fill the teapot with boiling water.

- Allow it to steep, covered, for 5 minutes. Stir up the infusion and taste the liquid to see if it is sweet enough.

- Strain into small glasses to serve (like juice glasses – this is what is traditional).

Note: Prepare a second infusion while the guests are enjoying the first. Add another teaspoonful of tea, a teaspoonful of dried mint – or some more sprigs of fresh mint – and 2 tablespoons of sugar to the pot. Add boiling water and allow to steep again.

Serbian Coffee

from Regina Kondo

Serbs actually call this Turkish coffee, whereas Greeks call it Greek coffee and Arabs will call it Arabic coffee! Everybody who makes coffee this way considers it to be a little part of their identity. The precise method (whether you add the coffee to cold water or to hot water, for example) will vary according to local tradition. Here you have the Serbian method. You need a little metal coffee pot that can go on the hob: it is like a jug with a long handle. Your coffee must be ground extra fine for this process.

- Put a cup of water and a teaspoonful of sugar in the pot and bring to the boil.

- When it is boiling, reserve a tiny bit of the water in a cup and stir a spoonful of very finely ground coffee into the water in the pot.

- Then add the reserved water back into the pot and place it back on the stove: just heat it until the drink foams – don't let it re-boil, or you will lose the lovely foam – and it is ready.

- Pour the rich dark coffee into your cup, let it settle, and enjoy it. (Don't stir – again, this will cause the foam to disappear.)

Note: For variation, add a cardamom pod to the water while it heats.

Korean Persimmon and Ginger Punch

In most of Asia it is impossible to have a conversation about food without hearing about the various health-giving properties of the ingredients. Koreans in particular will enthuse at great length about how their copious consumption of garlic, chillies and kimchi has made them one of the healthiest and most disease-free nations in Asia. Even when everyone around me seems to be coughing and sniffling with early autumn flu, I usually manage to escape by making daily potfuls of this warming, soothing persimmon punch.

Known as 'sujeonggwa' in Korea, this punch can be served hot or cold and is highly prized in Korea as an immune-system booster. The scent of the cinnamon and ginger simmering away will make your kitchen smell a bit like Christmas. Dried persimmons can be purchased at Asian and Middle Eastern stores.

(makes enough for several glasses)

2 litres water

2 large thumb-size pieces of ginger, peeled and thinly sliced

6 3-inch pieces of cinnamon bark or sticks

6 tbsp honey (or more to taste)

a handful of dried persimmons

a handful of pine nuts

- Place the water, ginger and cinnamon in a pot and bring to a boil. Simmer for 45 minutes or until the liquid is reduced by almost half and has a strong ginger and cinnamon flavour.

- Strain out the ginger and cinnamon and stir in the honey until dissolved.

- Add the persimmons and set the mixture aside to cool. Place in the fridge and chill well.

- Toast the pine nuts in a dry frying pan on medium-low heat until golden.

- Pour the punch into glasses and top each glass with a scattering of pine nuts.

Note: You can serve it cold but this punch is also delicious drunk hot as a kind of tea.

Tibetan Butter Tea

from Maki Spanoudis

This recipe is as made and explained to me by Ani Samten from the Spa Road Tibetan Buddhist Centre. I'm neither a tea fan nor a hot drink fan, but this really does the trick for me!

pu·er tea

milk

butter

salt

- Make the tea, either in a pot as normal, or in a saucepan.

- Add some milk and bring to the boil (you can make it fairly milky).

- Add a knob of butter and dash of salt and simmer for a few minutes.

INDEX

NOTES

Acknowledgements

Thanks to everyone who assisted in realising the different stages of the Food For Mood project. In no particular order, thanks to Ulrika Bygge, Bex Large, Pablo Antoli, Lynda Laird, Ramin Farajpour, Yvey Bailey, Bahia Dawlatly, Cecilia Bonilla, Sabine Werner, Elizabeth Cochrane, Sasha Dee, Sandhya Kaffo, Amanda Walker, Priya Commander, Claudia Young, Becka MacKay, Abdellah Smita, Shada Hussein, Christine Nolan, David Blazey, Kate Williams, Nick Smith, Asia Wieloch, Kathrin Kirrmann, Amos Phillips, Michelle Baharier, Rosemary Shrager and all those who have contributed to the workshops and cookbook, and more broadly to all those who share their time, energy and goodwill with CoolTan Arts, as volunteers, participants, staff, friends, visitors, funders, mentors and trustees: you all make this project worthwhile.

This project was only made possible by the generous support of the Peter Minet Trust, SLaM and Guys' and St Thomas' Charity.

Chapter frontispiece illustrations by Cathy Smart

Cover design by Cecilia Bonilla

Photographs by Pablo Antoli, Ramin Farajpour, Lynda Laird, Michelle Baharier, Elizabeth Cochrane, Cecilia Bonilla, individual recipe contributors and the collective CoolTan Arts group

CoolTan Arts is a mental health arts charity based in Southwark. It is run by and for people with mental distress, supported by the efforts of a huge number of volunteers. The charity exists to inspire well-being and creative participation in a diverse range of people through the production of quality art, and it enables people with mental distress to play a wider role in the community through public activities.

The Food For Mood project was conceived after participants raised the area of food as one which was important to them. Several creative activities have been organised as part of the project, including dietary advice sessions, storytelling and drama sessions, discussion about shopping locally for healthy food, and workshops linking art, writing and cookery.

CoolTan Arts' participants represent the diversity of the Southwark community. We hope that this book will provide inspiration, ideas and support to everyone it reaches, encouraging people to eat healthily and well in a way that is enjoyable and realistic.

If you have enjoyed reading and using this book, please think generously about the help you could offer by donating funds or time. Contact us via our website www.cooltanarts.org.uk.